Chicago's Famous Buildings

CHICAGO SUN-TIMES

Third Edition
Revised and Enlarged

Chicago's Famous Buildings

A Photographic Guide to the City's Architectural Landmarks and Other Notable Buildings

Edited by Ira J. Bach
With the Assistance of Roy Forrey

Contributions by
Carl W. Condit and Hugh Dalziel Duncan

The University of Chicago Press
Chicago and London

Publication of this book was made possible by generous grants from the Graham Foundation for Advanced Studies in the Fine Arts and from the City of Chicago.

The University of Chicago Press, Chicago 60637
The University of Chicago Press, Ltd., London

Published 1965; Second Edition 1969;
Third Edition 1980
Printed in the United States of America

84 83 82 81 80 5 4 3 2 1

Library of Congress Cataloging in Publication Data

Main entry under title:

Chicago's famous buildings.

Second ed. (1969) by A. S. Siegel.
Bibliography: p.
Includes indexes.
1. Architecture—Illinois—Chicago—Guide-books.
2. Chicago—Public buildings—Guide-books. 3. Chicago—Buildings—Guide-books. I. Condit, Carl W.
II. Duncan, Hugh Dalziel. III. Bach, Ira J.
IV. Forrey, Roy. V. Siegel, Arthur S., ed. Chicago's famous buildings.
NA735.C4C4 1980 917.73'11'044 79–23365
ISBN 0–226–03395–3
ISBN 0–226–03396–1 pbk.

Contents

Foreword

This third edition of *Chicago's Famous Buildings* is completely revised in all aspects—the listing of the buildings, their categorizing, and many of their descriptions.

The decade between the second and third editions has seen the addition of many outstanding buildings and the loss of several old ones. Fortunately, the net total is still one of the nation's outstanding collections of architecture—principally because the city was once home to such creative geniuses as Louis Sullivan, Daniel H. Burnham, John Root, Frank Lloyd Wright, and Ludwig Mies van der Rohe, and thus contains structures like the Rookery, the Reliance Building, the Auditorium, the Charnley House, the Robie House, and the 860–880 Lake Shore Drive Apartments.

Instead of grouping buildings according to merit in historic styles or buildings of the Chicago School, Prairie School, general interest, and recent buildings, as was done in previous editions, this edition arranges them by geographic area, discussing the oldest buildings in an area first and continuing to the present. The date given for each building is the date of completion, as nearly as can be determined. The several maps show the location of each building. This is done for the convenience of persons using the book as a guide.

Altogether 164 buildings and areas are listed now, as against 112 in the previous edition. Not only has the number of entries increased by 52, but also more than half the total number of entries are new. Wherever possible, the photographs by Richard Nickel and Arthur Siegel have been retained, their work having received international attention since their untimely deaths. We are also pleased to add the work of photographers Barbara Crane, Bob Thall, Phil Turner, Harold Nelson, Michael Peter Weinstein, Phylane Norman, Alice Sinkevitch, and Dan Wilson. Their specific credits are listed immediately after the Glossary.

Roy Forrey of the Commission on Chicago Historical and Architectural Landmarks has been my assistant throughout the preparation of this edition. In this capacity, he has revised some descriptions and prepared many new ones.

Professor Carl W. Condit has updated his work in the second edition, now entitled *"The Chicago School: . . . and Changing Forms."* Many of J. Carson Webster's descriptive texts from the previous editions have been retained, as has Wilbert Hasbrouck's material on the buildings in Oak Park and River Forest.

The maps for this edition were provided by the City of Chicago Department of Planning, City, and Community Development and were prepared by Lawrence Young.

Chicago's Famous Buildings is not meant to be a comprehensive guidebook to Chicago architecture. Rather, it highlights those buildings that have frequently been cited for their architectural or historical significance. We have drawn heavily on the work of the Commission on Chicago Historical and Architectural Landmarks, which recommends official landmark designations to the City Council of Chicago. The Commission has sponsored this third edition, as it did the earlier two. Most of the structures that have been designated as Chicago Landmarks because of their architectural significance have been included in this edition of *Chicago's Famous Buildings* (indicated by *CL* in the heading of the entry). Other structures that have been suggested for designation by the Commission's Advisory Committee have also been included. Additional structures included have been listed on the National Register of Historic Places, a federal program of landmark designation, or are located within districts listed on the Register (marked *NR*).

We are most grateful to the City of Chicago and the Graham Foundation for Advanced Studies in the Fine Arts for renewed financial support. Their help has enabled the University of Chicago Press to offer *Chicago's Famous Buildings* at a purchase price within reach of a larger segment of the public than would be possible otherwise.

Thanks are due the following persons for assistance and advice during the preparation of this revised and enlarged third edition: Irene Siegel for generously making available photographs from the previous editions; Carter Manny, director, Graham

Foundation, for making suggestions pertaining to the graphic design and photography; John Entenza, former director, Graham Foundation, for continuing his interest and advice during selection of buildings; Marshall M. Holleb, for his perspicacity and advice on technical matters; Lewis W. Hill, former commissioner of the Department of Planning, City, and Community Development, now chairman, Regional Transportation Authority, for early support; Thomas Kapsalis, former commissioner, Department of Planning, City, and Community Development, now commissioner of Aviation Planning, for continued support; Margaret O'Brien of the Illinois-Indiana Bi-State Commission and the staff of the Commission on Chicago Historical and Architectural Landmarks and its director, William M. McLenahan. The Chicago Architecture Foundation and the Landmarks Preservation Council deserve mention for the tremendous service they have done through their various programs to increase public awareness of Chicago's architecture.

We are grateful to Sandra K. Rollheiser of the Chicago Municipal Reference Library and to its librarian, Joyce Malden, for suggesting material used in the Bibliography.

Finally, this book is dedicated posthumously to Arthur Siegel, whose clarity of purpose and dedication as editor of the first two editions make this third one a reality.

Ira J. Bach

The Chicago School: Original Principles . . .

Hugh Dalziel Duncan

The buildings illustrated in this guide are part of the great cultural heritage of America. Chicago is the national, and indeed the world, capital for historical landmarks of modern architecture. Almost the whole history of what we call "contemporary design" can be examined in Chicago. For Chicago is the birthplace of modern architecture, and some of the buildings illustrated here are among the first, and greatest, examples of it. That is why architects come from all over the world to study these great buildings. Chicago is the urban center of the life and work of Frank Lloyd Wright and Ludwig Mies van der Rohe, who, along with Le Corbusier, are the great architects of our time. Another Chicagoan, Louis Henri Sullivan, was the master from whom Wright, Mies, and Le Corbusier drew inspiration in developing their talents and their understanding of the architect's role in society.

The architecture of the Chicago School was first considered a style among many styles. From 1890 until about 1920, it was thought of as commercial or industrial architecture. In the twenties, many critics dismissed the work of the Chicago School as representing a crude "commercial" style to be "refined" by other architects. Such architects, mostly classicists, were educated in European schools and worked with clients who were interested in beautiful buildings so long as the beauty was European, not American. Sullivan, it was admitted, had done some good ornament but this was really wasted, and even "out of place," on commercial buildings. But in the thirties, as the work of Le Corbusier and Perret in France, Behrens, Gropius, Mendelsohn, and Mies van der Rohe in Germany, Berlage and Dudok in Holland, and Frank Lloyd Wright in America began to be accepted as genuinely creative, even conventional critics were forced to admit that modern architecture might be more than a passing fad.

An order of architecture, unlike a style, expresses a way of life. It is the expression of the community, not simply that of a class or an individual. This community for Jenney, Adler, Root, Burnham, and Wright was the democratic community. For however the architects of the Chicago School differed on design and however they argued about the relationship of engineering and architecture, they all agreed that the only architecture worth having was a democratic architecture. Indeed, Sullivan taught that democracy *depended* on its architects as much as on its statesmen or businessmen. He argued, with deep and prophetic conviction, that until democracy produced a good architecture and good art, it could not produce a good life for its citizens. Thus from the very beginning modern architecture in Chicago was part of a search for a social philosophy of democracy, as well as a search for perfection of form.

But while it was easy enough to talk about a people's art and a democratic architecture, it was another matter to produce it. In both his buildings and his early talks to Chicagoans on architecture, Sullivan asked questions. What is the proper form for a democratic architecture, and what kinds of human relationships will be possible in this new architecture? He answered the first by proposing that whatever the use of a building, its form must follow its function—not a mechanical function, like a traffic flow, circulation of air, heating, lighting, etc., but *human* function. He thought that the architect must ask himself: How can I enhance the human satisfaction of acting within my building or the communities I design? If I design a house of prayer, how do I make prayer more significant? If I design a department store, how do I make shopping more pleasurable? If I design a factory, how do I make work healthy and pleasurable? If I design a tomb, how do I make the sorrowing family feel the serenity and peace of death as a memory of life?

This is what Sullivan meant by his constantly repeated phrase: "A building is an act." And it is also what he meant by insisting that a building, indeed all architecture, is a moral act because it is an aesthetic act. In his *Kindergarten Chats,* the record of the spiritual voyage of a young architect, Sullivan takes us on a walk through the streets of Chicago, his city of joy and sorrow. As we walk beside the master we discover that he reads buildings as we read character in the faces of people. Perhaps this is why he hated "phony" buildings. He thought a bank should look like a friendly meeting place for neighbors who had come to see each other and to talk over their problems with bank officials. A bank which looked like a fort, a great vault, a Roman temple, or a Gothic cathedral, enraged him. Why, he asked, does the banker not dress in a Roman toga and talk in Latin? And why, he asked over and over again, is the banker ashamed to be an American in his expression of a most characteristic American act—the exchange of money?

Outside of Chicago, few understood the significance of Chicago design. Adams, Norton, Bourget, and other visitors, during the years following the World's Columbian Exposition of 1893, told their readers and hearers that Chicago architecture, as indeed the whole city, was based on making money. And since the making of money, if not its possession, was, in the eyes of traditional aesthetes and the aristocracies of Europe and America, essentially an ignoble pursuit, how could culture, to say nothing of great art, come from business people? Easterners like Adams, Norton, Henry James, and Edith Wharton admitted that Chicago was "interesting" and even "significant," but its significance as a center of American art was simply beyond their comprehension. Their prejudice against business and their fear of the "alien" people pouring into American cities made it impossible for them to consider the relationships between money and art in anything but negative terms.

Such considerations are still difficult for many critics, professors, and historians. Yet if we are asked to make any sense out of what happened in Chicago and to think at all about why it produced the greatest architecture of our time, we must accept the fact that the greatest clients of Chicago architects were businessmen and their wives. Even Henry-Russell Hitchcock, whose *Architecture: Nineteenth and Twentieth Centuries* is the standard history of modern architecture, is obviously puzzled by how Chicago with "no established traditions, no real professional leaders, and ignorance of the architectural styles, past or present" produced the great architecture of our time—an architecture which owes its existence to "enlightened commercial patrons" who "demanded and often received the best architecture of their day." He is careful to make the point that it is a mistake to disregard the architectural genius of Chicago where the "strictly *architectural,* as well as the technical and social, significance of the major commercial monuments of the nineteenth century will be evident."

The contributions of Chicago engineers to the building art, to the creation of the city, and finally to the great Chicago Plan have often been told. Jenney's Home Insurance Building contained the first iron frame—the precursor of the steel cage. It was the first building whose walls were not load-bearing. But before the tall buildings could be built, foundations strong enough to carry their great weight in swampy soil had to be developed. Many new types of foundations were invented. Indeed, Chicago engineers were so advanced that the architects themselves were not able to keep up with them. Chicago grain elevators, which were built in the seventies on the banks of the River, used piling for foundations. Yet it was not until after 1890 that architects made common use of this type of foundation.

The new buildings of Chicago were not constructed by the city, by religious organizations, by educational institutions, or by private groups as palatial edifices. They were built by businessmen and they were built for profit. Even the Auditorium, which was the civic and cultural center of Chicago for many years, was built to make money. It was a civic center, a hotel, and an office building. It was financed like any other business venture on the expectation of profit. George M. Pullman built what he hoped would be a worker's utopia, but he made clear from the very start that, unlike the older American utopias founded by religious and cooperative groups, his utopia was strictly a business venture. The town of Pullman would provide that workers could be decently housed, fed, clothed, educated, entertained, and even worship God, at a profit to those who would build communities for them.

But the achievements of Chicago businessmen, the daring and organizing ability of her builders, and the brilliance of her engineers, great though they were, do not explain the Chicago School of architecture. For the genius of architecture is formed space, and however great the community and however abundant men, money, land, and people may be, they cannot produce a great architecture without the vision and imagination of the architect. When all is said and done, Chicago did not produce great architects because it gave them the opportunity to build a city or to rebuild a city destroyed by fire. Boston and San Francisco suffered from great fires. New York, in common with many other American cities, increased rapidly in size and population. Yet Chicago, and Chicago alone, from 1875 into the 1960s, has turned to great architects for her city plan, for her buildings, for her schools, and for her homes.

This happened because of the genius of Louis H. Sullivan, who struggled through his fifty-one years of practice in Chicago (1873–1924) to create in his buildings and to communicate in his writing an aesthetic of democratic architecture. This became known as "functionalism." The spirit of functional form was the expression of the social purpose of the building in its structure. Sullivan taught that each building must be unique. He never repeated his ornament. Each building had a "spirit" which must be respected. The expression of this spirit was as much a part of its "utility" as the plumbing. For only when the building *evoked* human satisfactions determined by the form itself could it become architecture. And only when such form could be reduced to some kind of principle could it become an order, and not merely a style of architecture.

Architectural principles are reached, as Sullivan, Root, Wright, and Mies van der Rohe taught, by asking: What is the chief characteristic of the structure? To answer this for the tall building, Sullivan said that the chief characteristic of the tall office building was its loftiness. This "is the very organ-tone in its appeal. It must be in turn the dominant chord in [the architect's] expression of it, the true excitant of his imagination. It must be tall, every inch of it tall. The force and power of altitude must be in it, the glory and pride of exaltation must be in it. It must be every inch a proud and soaring thing, rising in sheer exaltation that from bottom to top it is a unit without a single dissenting line. . . ."

The deeper principle underlying the character of the soaring tower is that the outward expression, structure, "design or whatever we may choose [to call it], of the tall office building should in the very nature of things follow the functions of the building. . . ." Architectural art has failed thus far, Sullivan taught, because it has not yet found a way to become truly plastic: "It does not yield to the poet's touch." It is the only art "for which the multitudinous rhythms of outward nature, the manifold fluctuations of man's inner being have no significance, no place." Greek architecture, great as it was, lacked rhythm because it was not related to nature, and because the great art of music had not been born. While possessing serenity, "it lacked the divinely human element of mobility." Gothic architecture, "with sombre ecstatic eye," evoked a copious and rich variety of expression, but it "lacked the unitary comprehension, the absolute consciousness and mastery of pure form that can come alone of unclouded and serene contemplation, of perfect repose and peace of mind."

Thus, while the Greek knew the "statics, the Goth the dynamics," of architecture, neither of them suspected the mobile equilibrium of it, because neither of them "divined the movement and stability of nature."

Failing in this, both have fallen short, "and must pass away when the true, the *Poetic Architecture* shall arise—that architecture which shall speak with clearness, with eloquence, and with warmth, of the fullness, the completeness of man's intercourse with nature and with his fellow men." The search for a new kind of movement in architecture, which Sullivan called "mobile equilibrium," is the clue to the aesthetics of the Chicago School of the past, as it is to Mies van der Rohe's work in the present.

When we look at Chicago's towers, we sense at once the tension between horizontal and vertical thrust. The resolution of this tension creates a "mobile equilibrium." As our eye travels up the massive flanks of the Monadnock, along the glass bays of the Reliance, the steel piers of 860–80 Lake Shore Drive, or the Inland Steel Company Building, we experience at once the soaring quality of the great tower. We are freed from earth and carried up into the sky. We are no longer earthbound: a new kind of power fills our being as a sense of movement—movement into the sky—sweeps over us. But the eye also rests on horizontal planes whose intersection with the vertical thrust arrests the eyes long enough to make our upward flight a rhythmic progression, not a headlong rush into space. The horizontal plane acts like a musical phrase.

Sometimes the spirit of form is horizontal; at other times it is vertical. Carson Pirie Scott, the Robie House, the Illinois Institute of Technology campus, accentuate horizontal planes. For Sullivan, Wright, and Jens Jensen, the great landscape architect, the horizontal line was the prairie line, the great rolling prairie of the Middle West which moved our artists so deeply. Wright, speaking for every middle western artist, said: "I loved the prairie by instinct as, itself, a great simplicity; the trees, the flowers, and sky were thrilling by contrast . . . the plain . . . serene beneath a wonderful sweep of sky." The horizontal plane becomes one of movement, flow, and continuity. And it is the human plane, the plane along which man walks with other men. The vertical thrust gives us a sense of power, but the horizontal brings us serenity and peace.

And this, in the last analysis, is the power of these great Chicago buildings. They are a humane expression of a new way of life—the modern urban community based on money and technology. They are humane because the architects of the Chicago School, from the first generation of the seventies and eighties to the third generation of the sixties in our century, have followed the teachings of their master, Sullivan. "With me," he said, "architecture is not an art, but a religion, and that religion but a part of democracy." In this spirit our best buildings and communities have been—and will be—designed. The love of the common man has been the glory of Chicago. The belief that only when he is decently housed can democracy survive has been the moral glory of our architecture. The conviction that he must be beautifully housed and sheltered has become the aesthetic credo of modern architecture. Who is to do this—the state, the businessman, or the powerful institutions of the democratic community itself—is by no means certain. But that it *must* be done is certain. For democracy cannot exist without good architecture, and good architecture in turn can be created only among men who walk the earth in freedom and dignity.

(1965)

The Chicago School: . . . and Changing Forms

Carl W. Condit

"For sheer commercial splendor," wrote architectural historian Reyner Banham, "Chicago is the rival of Baroque Rome." While one may suspect there is some measure of hyperbole in this dictum, it is nevertheless indicative of the international reputation the city enjoys for its achievements in the building arts. The earliest buildings recognizable as bearing a special Chicago stamp were erected around 1880; they marked the beginning of a movement later to be known as the Chicago School. The expression itself was first used by the architect and historian Thomas E. Tallmadge in an article published under the title "The Chicago School" in the April 1908 issue of *Architectural Record*. Tallmadge was referring to a more or less unified body of residential work designed by a group of young architects whose leader was Frank Lloyd Wright, at least up to his departure for Europe in 1909, and whose spiritual mentor was Louis Sullivan. Some thirty years later the Swiss historian Siegfried Giedion revived the term to represent the large multistory buildings of advanced design erected between 1880 and 1900. He recognized, as did Chicago architect Earl Reed some years before him, that the buildings in question constituted a distinct commercial style. To avoid confusion still another historian, H. Allen Brooks, coined the phrase "Prairie School" for the kind of work described in Tallmadge's article, thus reserving the original expression for the commercial architecture discussed in Giedion's influential *Space, Time and Architecture*. Although they are for the most part recognizably distinct, the two phases of the Chicago movement were closely related, and they overlapped one another for a number of years after the turn of the century.

The Chicago School, as we will employ the term in this essay, flourished chiefly over the thirty years from 1880 to 1910, while the high plateau of the Prairie School extended over the twenty years from 1900 to 1920. By the early years of the century the two schools had produced an original, indigenous, unified, yet highly diversified architecture for every kind of building—office skyscrapers, department stores, hotels and apartments, warehouses and factories, residences, schools, churches, and tombs. During the extraordinary decades of the eighties and nineties, the architects and engineers of Chicago developed the structural system of the contemporary multistory building and many of the essential forms of modern architecture. "Here is where it all began," as the editors of *Architectural Forum* once wrote.

From the beginning the Chicago School divided into two major streams, whose respective founders were William LeBaron Jenney and Louis Sullivan, with John Wellborn Root close behind the latter in his authority. Jenney was a strict utilitarian, a rationalist and empiricist who sought the most economical forms of building to satisfy the functional requirements. His aims were maximum efficiency and economy of construction, open interior space, and the maximum admission of natural light. The external form that grew out of this program is distinguished mainly by the articulated or cellular wall of "Chicago windows," a basic rectangular pattern corresponding in its geometry to the underlying frame of iron or steel and surmounting an open base of glass often treated like a continuous transparent screen. Sullivan and Root, however, tended to be subjective and romantic, architects who treated a building as a plastic object molded to give expression to philosophical ideas often remote in their sources from questions of practical utility. Sullivan, in particular, used the formal design of elevations to express philosophies of nature and democracy, or the strong empathic responses that the new structural technology aroused in him.

In spite of Jenny's narrow pragmatic approach, which was best realized in the Sears Roebuck Store (1889–91), his influence led to a great diversity of forms derived in their external appearance from the underlying rectangular cage of iron or steel. The most thorough exploration of the formal possibilities inherent in the Jenney program appears in the work of Holabird and

Roche, the most prolific of the Chicago architects during the heroic age. The classic design from their hands is the Marquette Building (1893–94), which offers an authoritative example of how sober functionalism and the steel skeleton can be transformed into a highly expressive commercial architecture. The underlying structure and its fireproof cladding are enclosed entirely in brick and terra-cotta. By means of narrow moldings on the sheathing of spandrels and wall columns and an intertwining repetitive ornament spread in low relief over entire surfaces at the corner bays, the pattern of huge rectangular cells is lifted from the level of a purely technical solution to that of a striking and unprecedented aesthetic form. Other variations on the theme of the cellular or articulated wall characterize later works of the same architects—the buildings of the Gage group (1898), the McClurg (1899–1900), the Chicago (1904), and the Brooks (1909–10), a closely unified series of designs, yet each exhibiting its own formal character.

Louis Sullivan, by contrast, approached architecture, not from the scientific and empirical, but from the personal and the philosophical standpoint. External form and internal decor were designed to embody ideas about man and nature and to express the psychological role of a building. In the steel-framed skyscraper, for example, the ruling characteristics were loftiness and upward motion, and these became motifs in the decorative scheme; in the big masonry block the materials for ornamental enhancement were often the weight of massive bearing walls and the rhythm of piers and arcades. Only two of Sullivan's works designed to the new urban scale survive in Chicago, but fortunately they stand among the best. The Auditorium Building (1887–89), the first great achievement of the partnership with Dankmar Adler and a true megastructure, still remains in a class by itself. The masonry bearing walls are divided horizontally into a massive base of rusticated granite, an intermediate section of smooth, strongly rising limestone piers, and a top floor set off by a lively rhythm derived from small windows closely set in triple groups. The idea was not to express the complex internal divisions of the huge structure—office block, theater, hotel—nor to express any structural technique, but to treat the elevations in a plastic way, urging the eye to move from static mass at the base to a light crown at the top in a quickening tempo. The interior of the theater is perhaps the supreme example in American architecture of decoration employed to define and accent the enclosing surfaces and their bounding lines in a huge, intricately shaped and subdivided volume.

In the Carson Pirie Scott Store (1899, 1903–4, 1906), Sullivan chose the articulated wall of what I have called the empirical mode because of the requirement for maximum natural light, but in his hands the simple rectangular geometry of the elevations is developed into the highest level of design by means of a skill in ornamentation that no later architect has been able to command. The base is a light screen of large display windows set in a cast-iron shell covered with an astonishingly rich, flowing, floral, and foliate ornament kept unobstrusive by very low relief. A similar ornament, reduced to the utmost delicacy, is disposed in narrow bands to enframe each window and to extend in continuous horizontal ribbons from end to end of the elevations at the sill and lintel lines of every story. Once again Sullivan began with functionalism but translated it into a purely formal program, the aim of which was to invite the attention of the passerby at the base, to define the rectangular cells in the wall above, and to intensify or even to exaggerate the long flowing lines of the structure. In no other commercial building can we find this union of subtlety and power.

The horizontal elongation of wide-bayed framing appears again in the huge reinforced-concrete warehouse designed by Schmidt, Garden and Martin for Montgomery Ward and Company and erected in 1906–8. By means of narrow moldings on the spandrels, the architects of the building deliberately intensified the natural horizontality of the long bands of massive concrete girders. The same motif distinguishes many houses from the hands of the Prairie School architects, among whom Wright stood preeminent. His masterpiece in the Prairie idiom is the Robie House, although here the total form is developed into a complex pattern of intersecting planes and volumes. A little more than fifty years after these various works were completed, the horizontal orientation of wide bays was again becoming prominent in the city's buildings, but they appeared then as unadorned geometric abstractions lacking in the aesthetic richness of Sullivan's and Wright's work.

The classic ancestor of the sculptural architecture that became common in the decades of the sixties and seventies is Burnham and Root's Monadnock Building (1889–91), which shows a refinement and simplification of the lively ornament of their earlier Rookery (1885–86). Root stood next to Sullivan as the kind of imaginative architect who could create vivid forms out of functional demands. The Monadnock is Root's masterpiece in Chicago. The austere geometry of this great masonry slab was raised to the level of a powerful aesthetic statement not by ornament, as would have been the case with Sullivan, but by literally shaping the inert brick mass into a kinetic image, conveying a strong impression of flowing, rhythmic movement. The key motif is the curved surface, which appears wherever two planes meet in a dihedral angle. The corners of the main block are developed into a rounded transition between walls, the curve revealing an expanding radius from bottom to top. The slight inward curve at the second-floor level is balanced by the outward flare of the parapet rising above the roof, and this is repeated at smaller scale near the top of each bank of projecting bays, or oriels. The soffit, or lower surface of the bank, literally flows through a reverse curve from the face of the oriel spandrel into the face of the massive wall below it. An epoch-making work in all respects, the Monadnock offers an authoritative lesson in how a gifted architect can translate technology into plastic art.

Projecting bays like those of the Monadnock were first adapted to the curtain walls of steel-framed commercial buildings by Holabird and Roche, but they were given a particularly clean, sharp-edged statement by Clinton J. Warren in the Congress Hotel. (Warren designed the original north block, completed in 1893, but Holabird and Roche followed his program in the later south wing, opened, as it now stands, in 1907.) The deep, solid piers of the Monadnock give way to a light curtain of glass and thin limestone veneer in the somewhat brittle multifaceted walls of the hotel.

The Reliance Building, designed and partly constructed in 1889–91 but completed in 1894–

95, may be regarded as a joint creation of Root and Charles B. Atwood of D. H. Burnham and Company. This remarkable building shares with the Carson store the honor of being the most impressive example of how aesthetic form may be created from the objective demands of utility and structure. It stands exactly at the opposite end of the spectrum from the Monadnock among works of the Chicago School. Again, subtle details constitute the special ingredient that gives life to these already elegant screens of glass and terra-cotta. Chicago windows set nearly in the same plane with the spandrels, proportions calculated with the utmost care, and broad projecting bays constitute the formal basis, but the final step in the transformation is the plastic treatment of the terra-cotta envelope. The moldings at the top and bottom of the spandrels, the circular medallions in low relief on their vertical faces, the clustered shafts of the highly attenuated mullions —these delicate embellishments not only add visual enrichment to street elevations that is rewarding in itself, but they also define and intensify the fundamental elements composing the thin cellular wall. It is instructive to compare the Reliance with the Brunswick Building (1963–65) one block to the west: the later work, from the office of Skidmore, Owings and Merrill, is a sophisticated technical solution to a collection of technical problems—technique uncelebrated, we might say; the earlier is a genuine work of urban architecture, possessed of *venustas* as well as *firmitas* and *utilitas* (to cite the Vitruvian triad).

The architects of the Chicago School were in various ways seeking to create new forms in response to new urban conditions. At the same time, the traditional eclectic or derivative architecture of the nineteenth century flourished in Chicago, as it did everywhere. With few exceptions, most notably the chief works of Henry Ives Cobb and H. H. Richardson and his successors, eclectic designs in Chicago stood well below the level of their counterparts in New York and other major cities of the East. This state of affairs changed rapidly after the turn of the century as the immense influence of the Ecole des Beaux-Arts in Paris began to penetrate the American hinterland. Typical office blocks in the twenty-story range that had been established before the end of the century are the combined office and headhouse building of LaSalle Street Station (1901–3), by Frost and Granger, and the Peoples Gas Company Building on Michigan Avenue (1910–11), one of the numerous products of the enormously prolific office of D. H. Burnham and Company. Both were done in the classical mode derived from various Renaissance precedents: the former restrained and sober, befitting the conservative railroad companies; the latter, richly clad in heavily molded terra-cotta, hoping to attract the eye of the consumer in a way favorable to the utility.

The promise of an improved quality of derivative architecture came with the design of hotel buildings. The Blackstone of Marshall and Fox and the LaSalle of Holabird and Roche, both erected in 1908–9, showed how thoroughly the leading Chicago architects had mastered the neo-baroque styles of Second Empire Paris and had adapted them to complex buildings whose twenty-two-story height clearly qualified them for the status of skyscrapers anywhere but in New York. (The LaSalle has been demolished, victim to the rage for degrading the Loop.)

The high-rise hotel and apartment building in Chicago, designed in the manner appropriate to the affluent, self-indulgent, comfort-loving dweller or traveler in the twentieth-century city, was virtually the creation of Benjamin Marshall and the firm of Marshall and Fox. The Blackstone, the Drake, and much of the Gold Coast survive to teach us how good architecture could retain its virtue while serving the ends of luxury and opulence.

The office building in the classical mode, still limited to the twenty-two-story height and the blocklike silhouette required under the old zoning ordinances, came of age with the Insurance Exchange (1911–12), another design from D. H. Burnham and Company and the largest office building in Chicago at the time. Enameled brick and terra-cotta have preserved the white sheathing of the Exchange even in Chicago's polluted air, so that one can see in a reasonably pure state how the best of corporate classicism was meant to appear, complete with colonnades at top and bottom. The promise implied by prewar buildings like the Exchange suddenly burst into full flower when the opening of the double-deck Michigan Avenue Bridge in 1920 provided the proper setting for the great bravura performance of Chicago architecture. The Wrigley Building (1919–21; annex, 1923–24), the work of Graham, Anderson, Probst and White, was to outclass all competitors in splendor, and architects have wisely refrained from trying to improve on its superbly controlled extravagance. The Wrigley differs from all its predecessors by virtue of its division into two distinct but well-unified parts, a lower block surmounted by a slender tower. The exterior design of the building is unashamed hedonism, sheer visual drama to excite the eye, the details of which were suggested by the Giralda Tower of Seville Cathedral and adapted by the architects with consummate skill to the requirements of the steel-framed skyscraper. The unique contribution of the United States to the urban environment was now ready to spring upward in other radically altered and still higher forms.

If the Wrigley could not be improved, it could at least be matched by an architectural dress of a different provenance. The owners of the *Chicago Tribune,* planning a new home for the paper and holding equally attractive property on the opposite side of Michigan Avenue, decreed an international competition in 1922 to insure that they would get the best. The first prize, announced in December of that year, went to Raymond Hood and John Mead Howells, and the structure based on their design was erected in 1923–25. The final form of this celebrated and endlessly controversial work, drawn from the Butter Tower of Rouen Cathedral, was based on an exhaustive study of all the features that are visible in the tower—the overall silhouette; the proportions of structural, quasi-structural, and external utilitarian elements; the relations of all these among themselves and to the basic form; and the ornamental details. In this way the most controversial feature and the one that most aroused Sullivan's exasperation, the ring of buttresses at the top, was chosen on a strictly formal basis, primarily to provide an open and graceful transition from the main shaft to the slender tower above it.

The building that stands diagonally opposite the Tribune at the Michigan Avenue–Wacker Drive–Chicago River intersection is the London Guarantee (1922–23), an elegant work from the hand of Alfred S. Alschuler based on a scholarly reading of Renaissance precedents. It stands as a necessarily sober balance to the flamboyance of the two towers on the north side of the river. The fourth skyscraper in this four-cornered group of prizewinners is known only by its address, 333 North Michigan Avenue. Erected in 1927–28 as the last major design from the office of Holabird and Roche, the 333 is another epoch-making work in the turbulent history of Chicago architecture. Its north elevation was derived from Eliel Saarinen's second-prize entry in the Tribune competition, and the architects' simplified revision of Saarinen's work made the 333 building the first Chicago skyscraper designed in the Art Deco mode. It was followed by three masterworks in the new style that were created by Holabird and Root and erected almost simultaneously in the frenzy of building activity that characterized the extravagant decade before the crash of 1929 brought it to its ignominious end.

The Palmolive (now Playboy; 1928–29) reveals the strongly marked setbacks that were required by the most recent changes in the zoning ordinance. The vigorous play of prismatic volumes is intensified by the device of recessing alternate bays in rectangular grooves or channels, which are relatively shallow in the lower blocks but deeply indented in the graceful tower that completes the strong upward thrust of the building. The visual consequence of both the offsets and the indentations is a rhythmic counterpoint of projecting and receding surfaces, embodied in broad bands of limestone sheathing, which constitutes one of the chief distinguishing features of Art Deco architecture.

The second of the triumvirate, the original Daily News (now Riverside Plaza) Building, constructed at the same time as the Palmolive, exhibits another variation on the fundamental volumetric forms, since the emphasis is less on height or verticality than on horizontal elongation. The primary element in this interplay of rectangular prisms is a narrow slab, its long axis extending parallel to the river, set off by low blocks in the form of advancing wings at the ends of the central volume. The Daily News was the first building in Chicago to be erected on railroad air rights: the structure and its associated plaza stand over the tracks in the north half of Union Station (a severely Doric monument, we might add, from the hand of Graham, Anderson, Probst and White, its great concourse building now gone).

In the Board of Trade Building (1929–30) Holabird and Root returned to the skyscraper tower, which in this case is their most impressive design not only in itself, but also by virtue of its spectacular setting at the foot of the LaSalle Street canyon. The building is characterized by the symmetrical and rhythmic setbacks of the Palmolive, though with loftier and slenderer forms. They are closely unified with the powerful upward sweep of the central bays, which rise swiftly in diminishing steps to the pyramid roof. At its apex stands the statue of Ceres to remind us of the enduring authority of classical myth, surviving at least until abstract art swept away all emblematic, allegorical, and symbolic sculpture, leaving the city poorer for the loss. The Civic Opera House and its associated office tower (now the Kemper Insurance Building), erected like so many of its fellows in 1928–29, brought the office of Graham, Anderson, Probst and White once again to prominence. With respect to style, the Civic Opera might be categorized as conservative Art Deco embodying decorative principles derived from the French Renaissance. It is the best example among buildings designed for both commerce and art of emblematic and symbolic ornament. The details are drawn chiefly from the musical arts—the lyre, the trumpet, and the laurel wreath, the last an attribute of Apollo, the god of knowledge and art.

The public buildings that reflect the intellectual and artistic life of Chicago shared in the creative surge of the 1920s. Several of the city's cultural institutions are scattered through the lakefront parks, from the Chicago Historical Society and the Academy of Sciences in Lincoln to the Museum of Science and Industry in Jackson, but the greatest number are stretched out in a great L-shaped group along the two sides of Grant Park. Together they constitute the largest, oldest, architecturally richest, and most diversified cultural center in the United States—from north to south and west to east, the Public Library (1897), now the Cultural Center, the Art Institute (1893),

Orchestra Hall (1904), the Field Museum (1920), the Shedd Aquarium (1929), and the Adler Planetarium (1930). The Field Museum of Natural History takes us back at its inception to the heroic years of Daniel Burnham, whose office prepared the original plans in 1906 for a site at the location of the future Buckingham Fountain in Grant Park. There followed a long controversy over the appropriate place for the building, finally resolved with a choice of site along East Roosevelt Boulevard, immediately south of the park. Before construction was initiated in 1915, the work of detailed design had passed to old D. H.'s successor firm, Graham, Burnham and Company. The huge Ionic temple, possessed of a genuine majesty, to be sure, but somewhat coldly and heavily monumental at the same time, was finally opened to the public in 1920. Still another Burnham successor—Graham, Anderson, Probst and White—was then involved in the completion of working drawings.

The John G. Shedd Aquarium (1928–29) is a considerably more restrained and elegant work from the Graham office. A Greek cross in plan, the white marble structure, surmounted by a pyramidal skylight, is finished in details drawn from the Doric order and carefully subordinated to the fundamental geometry of the smooth-walled enclosure. The soft yet sparkling texture of the marble veneer and the formal simplicity are exactly appropriate to the aquarium's magnificent lakeshore setting. The Max Adler Planetarium (1929–30), designed by Ernest Grunsfeld, Jr., and standing farthest to the east along the city's lakefront fill, is perhaps the last building of which the entire envelope constitutes a work of true symbolic form. Three similar dodecagonal prisms rise in diminishing tiers to the base of the hemispherical dome, the twelve-sided volumes representing the twelve months and their associated zodiacal signs, the dome a symbol of the celestial sphere whose luminaries are simulated on its inner surface. The geometric purity, the subtle ornamental detail, the rich dress of polished rainbow granite, the levels of meaning with roots in classical antiquity—these brought Grunsfeld the Gold Medal of the American Institute of Architects in 1930, an honor that no one better deserved. The decorative elements one finds in the opera house and the planetarium, drawn from musical arts, cosmology, and classical myth, brought the architecture of expressive and symbolic meaning to an end. The triumph of international modernism that eventually followed may have given us striking forms that appeal to the eye, but it is highly questionable whether they can appeal to the mind and the heart.

The depression of the 1930s, followed immediately by the Second World War and the postwar economic adjustments, brought a twenty-year hiatus to new construction in the United States, and when building was resumed around 1950 the once heretical doctrines of Le Corbusier and the Bauhaus everywhere triumphed. Yet the new architecture in Europe could offer no parallel to the Chicago movement at its height. When the leading pioneers in France and Germany began to win attention, even their best designs seemed coldly abstract beside the great richness and variety of Chicago architecture. In one of the ironies of our cultural history, however, when urban architecture revived in the United States, it did so under the impetus of European importations. It was an old story—the distrust of native achievements, the belief that Europe must always be the fountainhead of new artistic and intellectual creations. The early work of the European avant-gardists revealed an undeniable mastery of contemporary structural techniques and their formal possibilities, but it was a prime misfortune that the so-called International Style should have swept everything else before it.

The gospel reached Chicago through Mies van der Rohe, who was invited to assume the directorship of the school of architecture at the Armour Institute of Technology in 1938. The local embodiment of the new dispensation, an amalgam of neo-Chicago and the European avant-garde, came with Mies's Promontory Apartments (1948–49), the first of a long series of major commissions for apartment and office towers that kept the architect busy until his death in 1969. The naked structuralism of Promontory, its elevations reduced to an exposed concrete frame, brick spandrels, and window groups filling the bays from column to column, was fortunately not congenial to the Miesian temperament, and the architect turned to the welded steel frames and delicate vertical tracery that became the hallmark of his best skyscrapers. The latter was a simple device, but it brought a changing pattern of light and shadow to the neutral glass screens, and simultaneously expressed the sharp-edged clarity and mathematical rigor of steel framing. The archetypal form appeared in apartment buildings at 860–880 North Lake Shore Drive (1949–52), received a particularly eloquent statement in Crown Hall at the Illinois Institute of Technology (1955–56), and reached its high point in the three buildings of the Federal Center (1961–74).

Mies's pervasive influence in Chicago began to manifest itself as soon as the construction drought ended in the Loop. The essentials of the original Chicago tradition reemerged with a Miesian overlay in the work of the office of Skidmore, Owings and Merrill. Their Inland Steel Building, at Monroe and Dearborn streets (1955–57), is a *tour de force* in the expression of welded steel framing. The nineteen-story glass prism contains no interior columns, the primary bearing elements being seven pairs of columns located outside the planes of the long elevations. The floors are carried on transverse girders of 58-foot clear span, a characteristic which makes the Inland Steel the first of the wide-bayed structures that began to dominate high-rise building in Chicago.

It required the combined talents of three large architectural offices to carry the principle to its ultimate statement. C. F. Murphy Associates, associated with the Skidmore group and Loebl, Schlossman and Bennett, reached the climax in their staggering design for the Chicago Civic Center, constructed in 1963–65 on the block bounded by Washington, Dearborn, Randolph, and Clark streets. The 648-foot tower—the highest in Chicago at the time of its completion—is carried on sixteen primary columns set for a maximum span of 87 feet. This unprecedented spacing dictated a floor-framing system of trusses with a uniform depth of 5½ feet. The massive elements of the steel skeleton are left unpainted on the exterior, the self-weathering metal allowed to oxidize to an impenetrable patina of dark red-brown. There is something almost brutal in this assertion of technical virtuosity, yet it is a magnificent celebration of engineering on an overwhelming scale.

Two novel essays in reinforced-concrete construction further reflected the innovative spirit of the 1960s. Across the street from the plaza of the Civic Center stands the Brunswick Building, constructed at the same time as its neighbor to the north. Another triumph of Skidmore engineering, the Brunswick was the largest building at the time of its construction with external walls built up as a load-bearing framework of slender columns and girders. Standing in absolute contrast to the ruling rectangular mode are the two towers of Bertrand Goldberg's Marina City, erected in 1960–64 as a succession of circular floors carried on a cylindrical core and two rings of circumferential columns. This unprecedented form offers a number of advantages in structural behavior and the efficient use of space and materials, although certainly comfortable interior planning is not one of them. The chief visual interest of the towers arises from the presence of a cantilevered semicircular balcony projecting from every segmental bay, which gives the buildings the lively appearance of a vertical succession of flower petals. Goldberg made the scalloped cylinder his particular trademark, adapting it to hospital buildings as well as residential skyscrapers.

Although its concrete structure is well hidden, the immense volume of Lake Point Tower (1965–68) is an even more spectacular example of curved forms in place of the traditional planes. Designed by John Heinrich and George Schipporeit, standing to a height of seventy stories close to the water at the base of Navy Pier, this behemoth achieved still other records: at the time of its completion it was the highest apartment building in the world and the highest reinforced-concrete structure. More arresting than its height, however, is its rounded three-lobed plan, a unique form suggested by a project that Mies proposed in 1921 for a Berlin skyscraper. The continuously curving surfaces of glass carried in a light metal armature represents the pure Miesian idiom uncluttered by later novelties.

The commanding lakeside tower, easily discerned up and down the shoreline to a distance of twenty miles in either direction, ushered in a decade of architectural novelties without precedent in form, structural character, and, above all, size. The First National Bank Building, constructed at the geometric center of the Loop in 1965–69, led the way among the giants by opening a year earlier than its nearest competitor. The joint creation of C. F. Murphy Associates and the Perkins and Will Partnership, its sixty-story, 800-foot height easily dominates every skyscraper in the city's core. The most striking features of the building, and another unique experiment in structural geometry, are the inward curving surfaces of the long elevations, ponderously accented by the huge external columns. This shape was adopted as the most aesthetically satisfactory solution to the problem of diminishing floor areas from the public space at street grade to the offices at mid-level and above. The architectonic treatment of the long elevations comes directly from the articulated wall that was common among the buildings of the original Chicago School.

While the planning and construction of the First National were under way, the office of Skidmore, Owings and Merrill was busy designing buildings marked by the first fundamental innovation in structure since the days of the early iron-framed skyscrapers in Chicago. The crucial problem in the construction of all high buildings is that of bracing the frame against the bending and twisting action of the wind. Skidmore engineer Fazlur Khan was the leading figure in the development of the technique that transformed the wall frames themselves into rigid structures able to resist wind loads by themselves, without any dependence on the complex and costly bracing devices that are ordinarily distributed throughout the entire framework.

The first building in Chicago to embody the new system clearly reveals the essential characteristic of its structure. The Hancock Building (1965–70) looks like an elongated rigid cage of tapering bridge trusses, which is exactly what it is. A powerful and indeed overwhelming technology is left to speak directly for itself: the architect's choice lay between one technique or an equivalent of somewhat different form, and he chose not to go beyond the unadorned facts of structure. Variations on the braced tubular cantilever, as it came to be called, soon appeared, the particular form depending on the type of rigid, wind-resistant truss employed for the wall frames. For the Sears Tower (1970–75), the Skidmore office adopted the Vierendeel truss (characterized chiefly by the absence of diagonal members) for the nine rigidly interconnected tubes that rise to varying heights, the two at the center of the cluster reaching 110 stories and 1,450 feet, to make the tower at present (1980) the highest building in the world. The dark, neutral screen that clothes the Sears giant is neither the revelation of technology nor a plastic, expressive, or even a patterned form, with the consequence that the finished building is most unsatisfactory as visual art. It would seem, again, that the aim of the architect is to discover the most appropriate technical solution and to stop at that point, considering his work complete.

To elucidate the full meaning of Chicago's contribution to the development of modern architecture would require an extensive historical and critical analysis. It is possible, however, to get at the fundamental character in a few generations. The great historical styles of architecture, as these appear in monumental works such as ecclesiastical and civic buildings, may be regarded in essence as the symbolic images of some kind of cosmos—divine, natural, political, or in a few cases all of them together, depending on the views of the age. In the absence of any public agreement on the nature of the encompassing order, modern architecture has tended to recapitulate the history of the Chicago School in continuing its two basic approaches to architectural form. The dominant one in recent years remains what it was at the end of the nineteenth century—namely, the empirical, rational, structuralist design that eventuates either in the articulated wall derived from the steel cage or in the neutral screen which seems so much like the Platonic abstraction of a building. This form arises entirely from the exigencies of utilitarian and structural requirements.

In recent years, however, there has grown up an increasingly potent rebellion against what is seen as the sterility of the ruling mode. If these heretical movements can be said to have a founder, he is probably Harry Weese, who began to break away from the Miesian authority in the design of apartment buildings erected from the mid-fifties on. By the next decade he was producing work in a more sculptural and plastic mode, or in richer colors, than one could ever find in the monastic severity of Mies and his followers. At the same time he moved to the front rank in the often bitter struggle to preserve the foremost achievements of Chicago's great cultural heritage and to return them to working use in the urban fabric. Other architects went further in either a subjective or a neotraditional direction. The human scale and the warmth of fine brickwork returned in the row houses and walk-up apartments of Jack Levin–Ezra Gordon Associates and the comparatively young office of Booth and Nagle. Perhaps the most imaginative of all the new generation is Stanley Tigerman, who, after looking upon years of solemnity and visual self-denial in the local architectural scene, has introduced elements of the capricious, the whimsical, and the ironic into architecture.

The promise of the future appears to lie in the direction marked out by these men, but the big firms—the palace architects, so to speak—show no intention of giving up any of the principles that have guided them through the years. Ribbon windows à la Erich Mendelsohn in the days of the Weimar Republic may take the place of neutral curtains, but the essential forms remain the same. Technical details are used as expressions of the mathematical and scientific concepts underlying the structure. The emotional impact derived from such buildings arises mainly from the evocation of kinesthetic images; the experience they offer is at best a formal intensification of that provided by engineering works such as bridges, dams, and other pure structural revelations. The empirical or rational stream in Chicago architecture belongs to a mode that seems increasingly poverty-stricken. Unless there is a remarkable burgeoning of creative ability, one finds it difficult to escape the conclusion that the high tides of Chicago building rose long ago, particularly in those two marvelous decades that began respectively in 1890 and 1920.

(1980)

Maps

METROPOLITAN ORIENTATION MAP

This orientation map of the metropolitan area of Chicago is shown with its network of expressway systems providing access to outlying subject sites. A trip to the most distant location is approximately thirty-three miles from State and Madison streets, and is easily driven by way of routes shown.

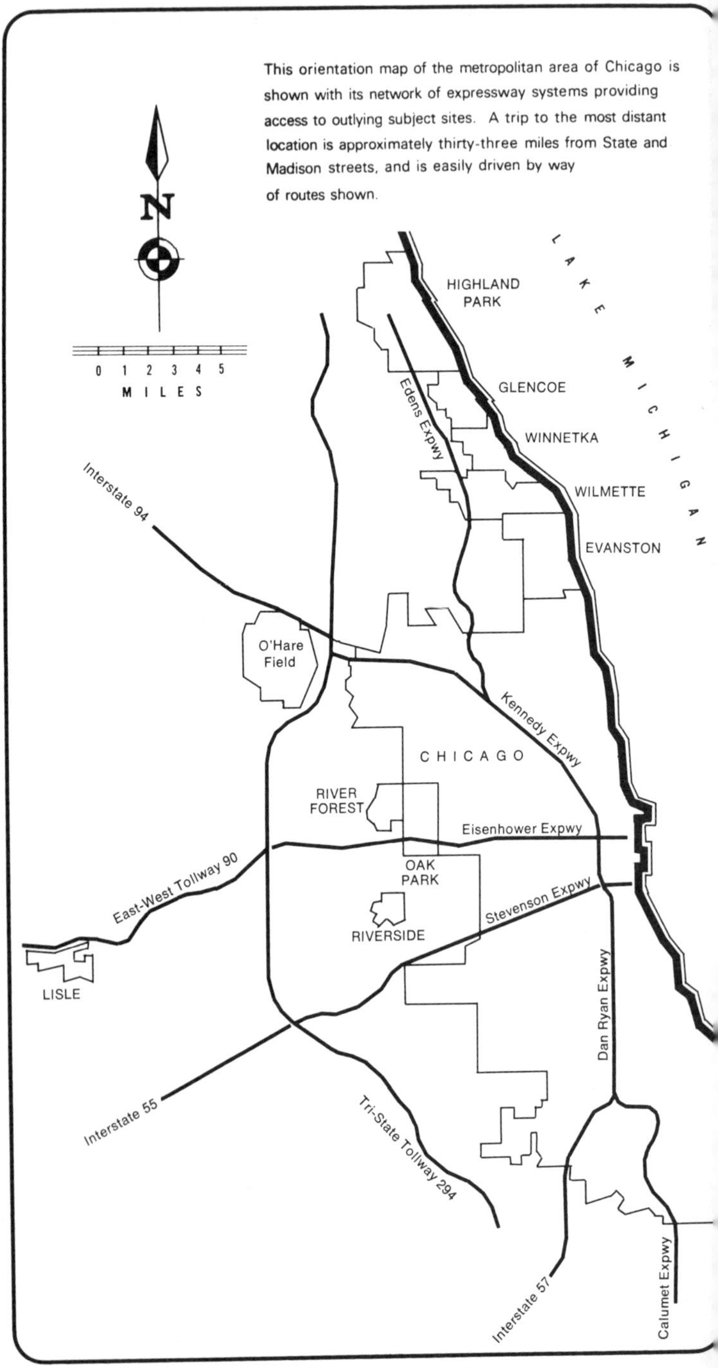

CITY OF CHICAGO AREA INDEX

This Area Index map groups sites that fall within the City of Chicago into six basic areas: Far North, Near North, Central, Near West, Near South and Far South. Scattered sites shown will appear within appropriate areas on map pages that follow.

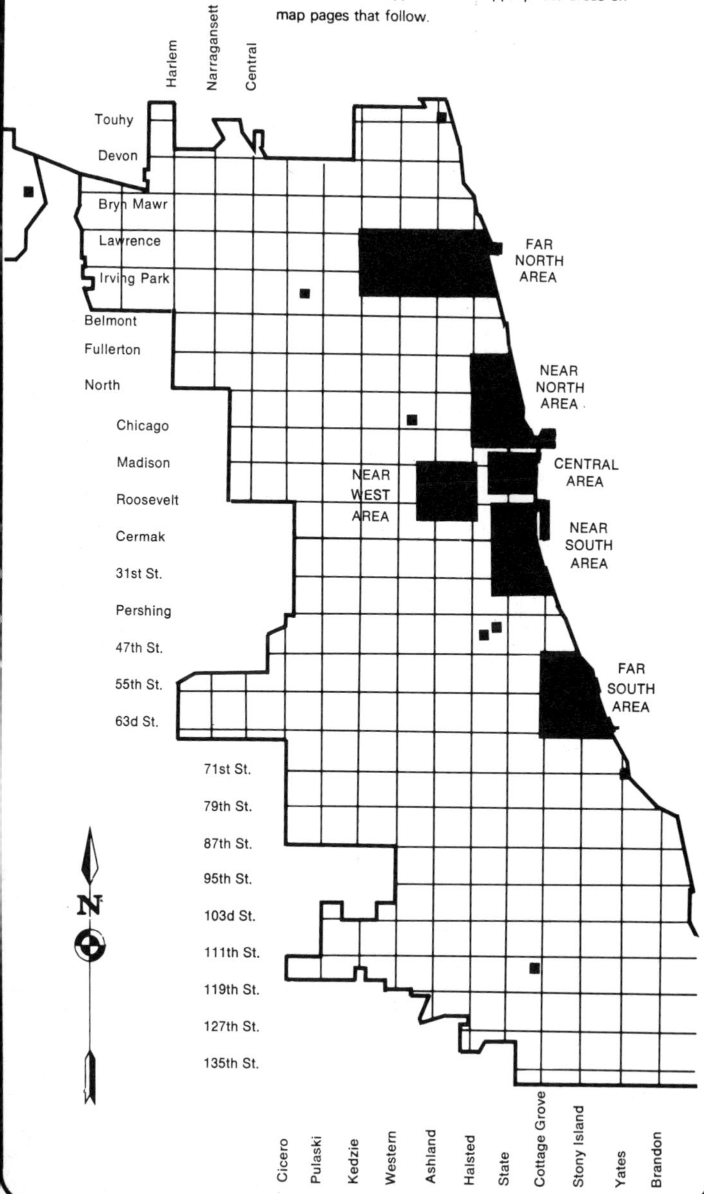

CENTRAL AREA

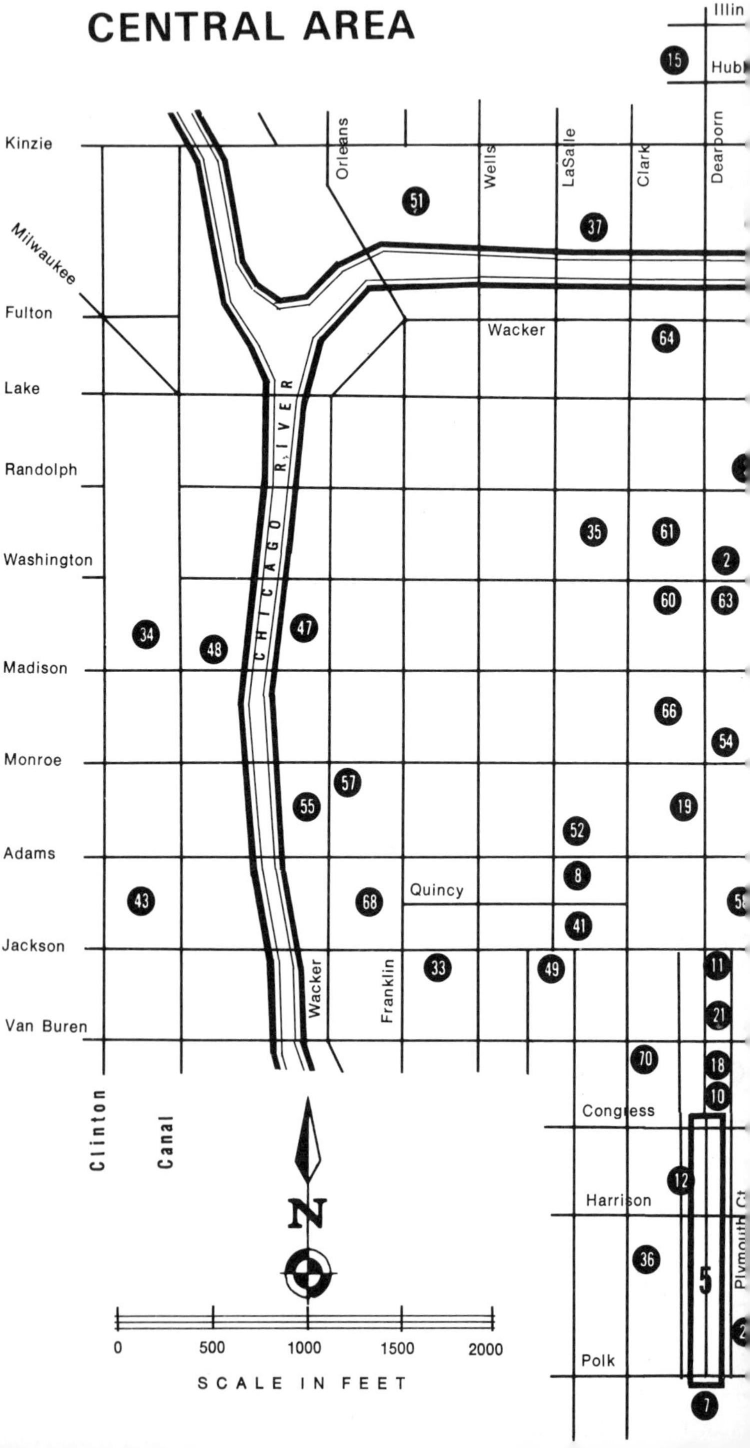

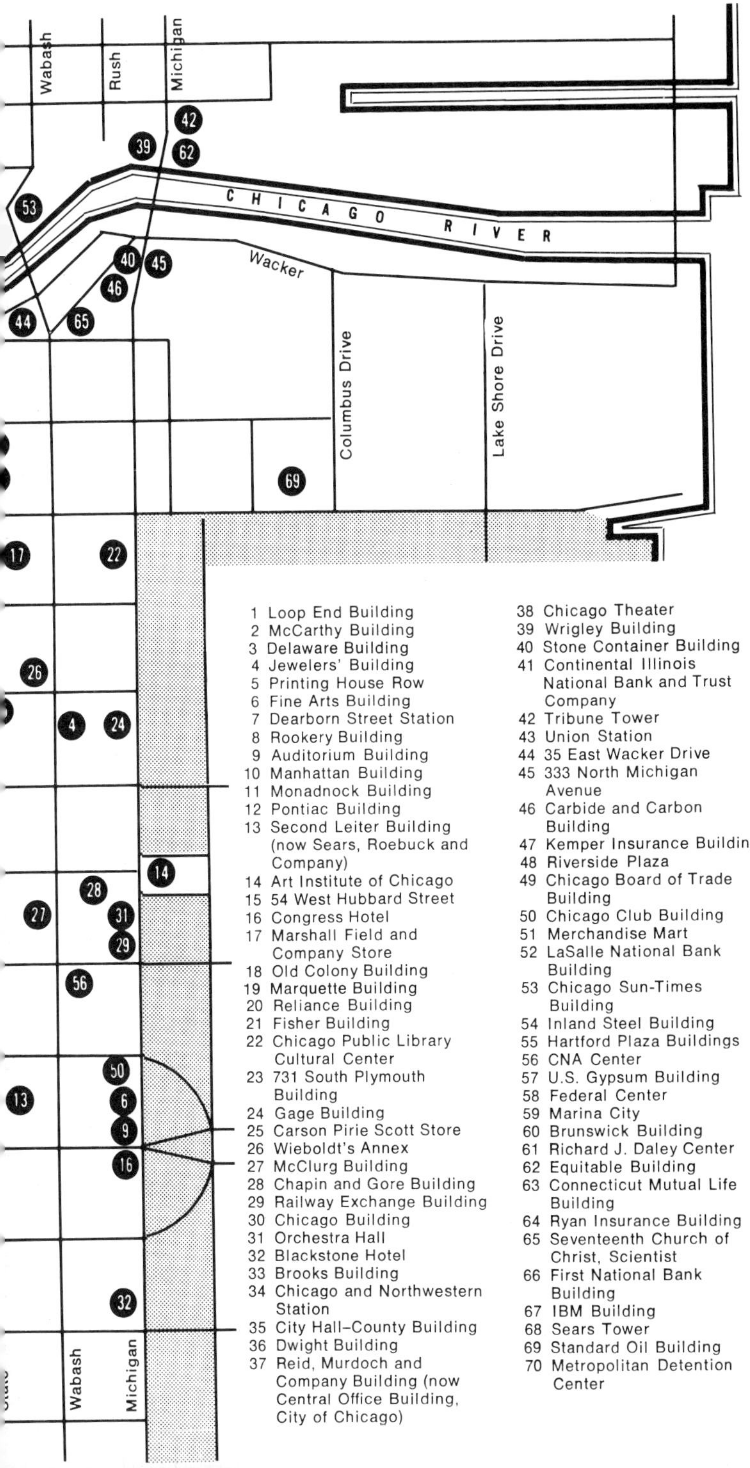

1 Loop End Building
2 McCarthy Building
3 Delaware Building
4 Jewelers' Building
5 Printing House Row
6 Fine Arts Building
7 Dearborn Street Station
8 Rookery Building
9 Auditorium Building
10 Manhattan Building
11 Monadnock Building
12 Pontiac Building
13 Second Leiter Building (now Sears, Roebuck and Company)
14 Art Institute of Chicago
15 54 West Hubbard Street
16 Congress Hotel
17 Marshall Field and Company Store
18 Old Colony Building
19 Marquette Building
20 Reliance Building
21 Fisher Building
22 Chicago Public Library Cultural Center
23 731 South Plymouth Building
24 Gage Building
25 Carson Pirie Scott Store
26 Wieboldt's Annex
27 McClurg Building
28 Chapin and Gore Building
29 Railway Exchange Building
30 Chicago Building
31 Orchestra Hall
32 Blackstone Hotel
33 Brooks Building
34 Chicago and Northwestern Station
35 City Hall–County Building
36 Dwight Building
37 Reid, Murdoch and Company Building (now Central Office Building, City of Chicago)
38 Chicago Theater
39 Wrigley Building
40 Stone Container Building
41 Continental Illinois National Bank and Trust Company
42 Tribune Tower
43 Union Station
44 35 East Wacker Drive
45 333 North Michigan Avenue
46 Carbide and Carbon Building
47 Kemper Insurance Building
48 Riverside Plaza
49 Chicago Board of Trade Building
50 Chicago Club Building
51 Merchandise Mart
52 LaSalle National Bank Building
53 Chicago Sun-Times Building
54 Inland Steel Building
55 Hartford Plaza Buildings
56 CNA Center
57 U.S. Gypsum Building
58 Federal Center
59 Marina City
60 Brunswick Building
61 Richard J. Daley Center
62 Equitable Building
63 Connecticut Mutual Life Building
64 Ryan Insurance Building
65 Seventeenth Church of Christ, Scientist
66 First National Bank Building
67 IBM Building
68 Sears Tower
69 Standard Oil Building
70 Metropolitan Detention Center

NEAR NORTH AREA

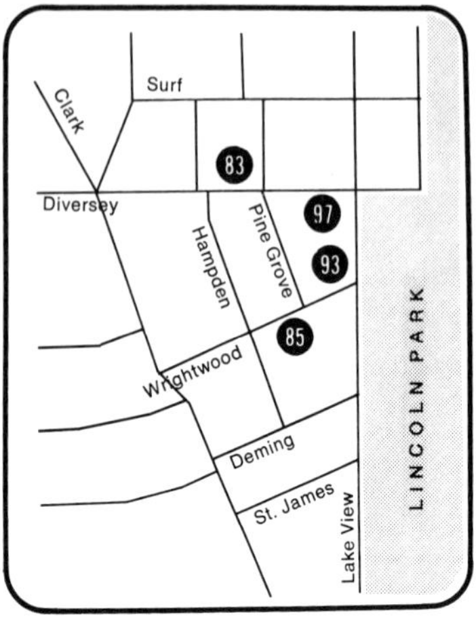

71 Episcopal Cathedral of St. James
72 Old Chicago Water Tower
73 Holy Name Cathedral
74 Old Town Triangle District
75 Mid-North District
76 Astor Street District
77 McCormick Row House District
78 Nickerson Residence
79 Charnley House
80 Fortnightly of Chicago
81 Newberry Library
82 Second Chicago Historical Society Building
83 Brewster Apartments

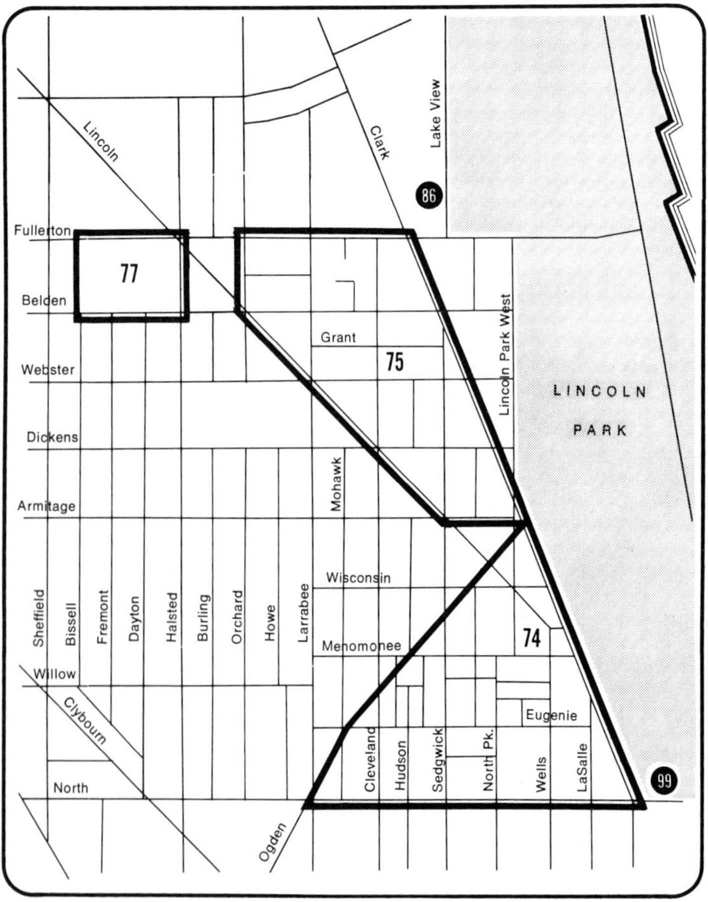

NEAR NORTH AREA

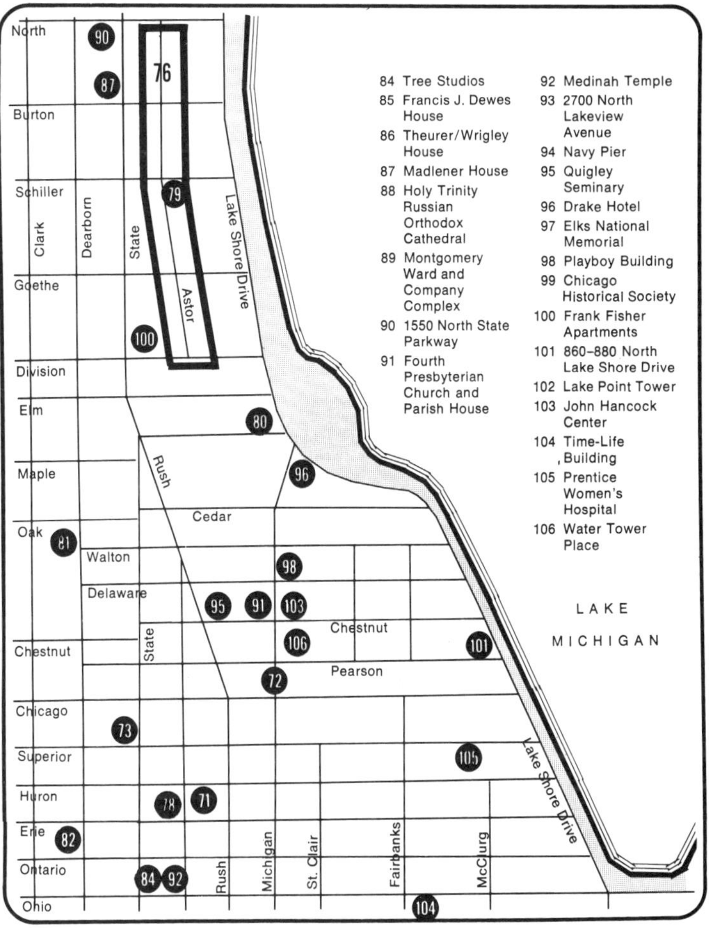

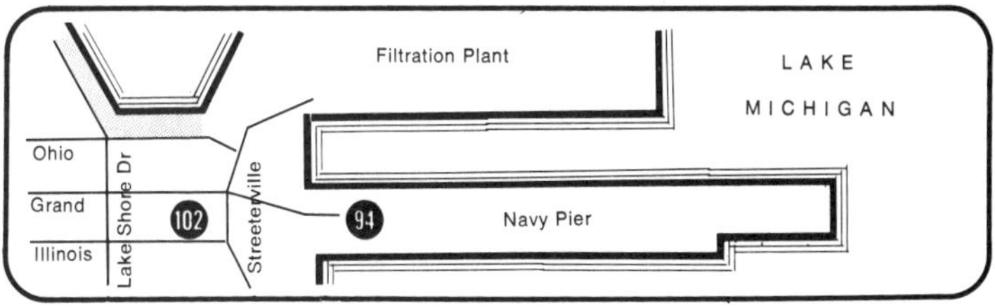

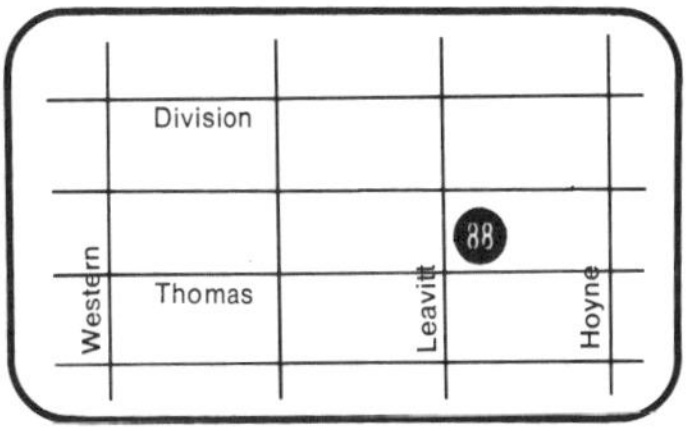

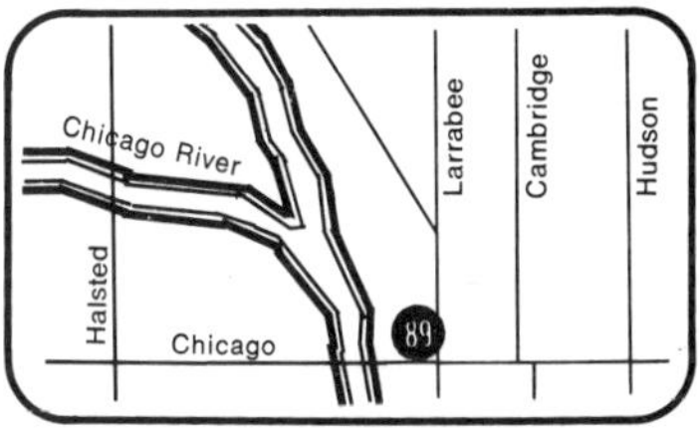

NEAR WEST AREA

107 St. Patrick's Church
108 Jane Addams's Hull House and Dining Hall
109 Holy Family Church and St. Ignatius
110 Jackson Boulevard District
111 Schoenhofen Brewery Building
112 University of Illinois Chicago Circle Campus
113 Rush University Academic Facility
114 Illinois Regional Library for the Blind and Physically Handicapped

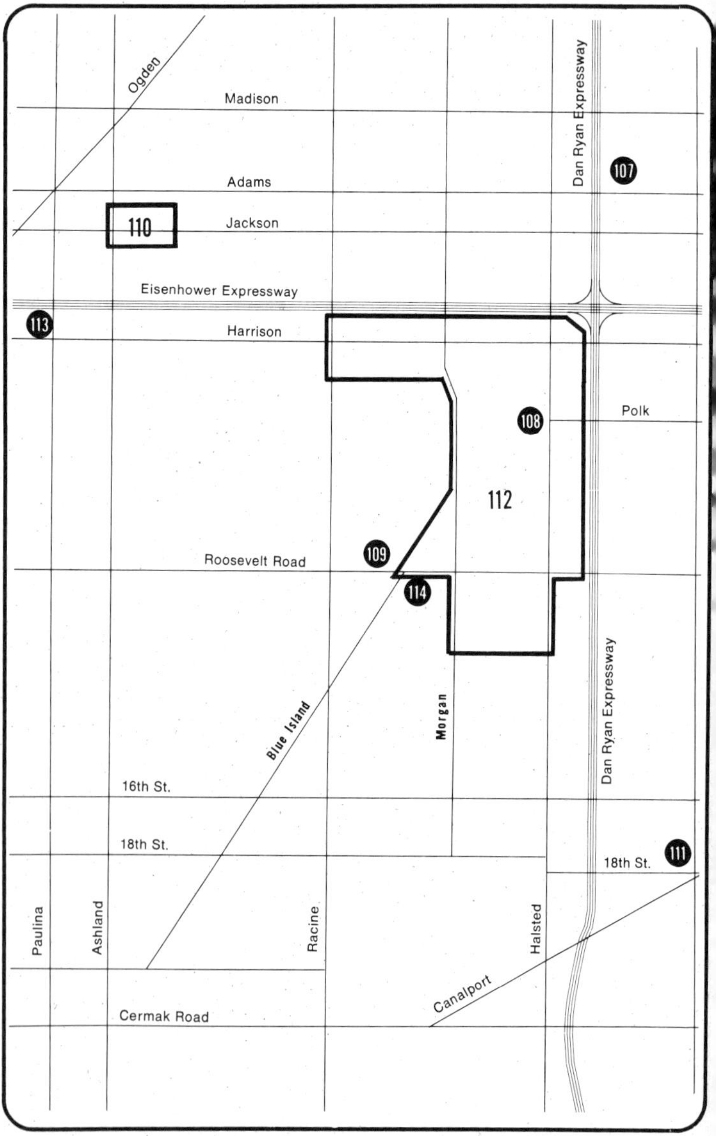

NEAR SOUTH AREA

115 Prairie Avenue Historic District
116 Henry B. Clarke House
117 Second Presbyterian Church
118 John J. Glessner House
119 R.R. Donnelley and Sons Building
120 Field Museum of Natural History
121 Park Buildings, Fuller Park
122 John G. Shedd Aquarium
123 Max Adler Planetarium
124 On Leong Chinese Merchants Association
125 Illinois Institute of Technology
126 McCormick Place

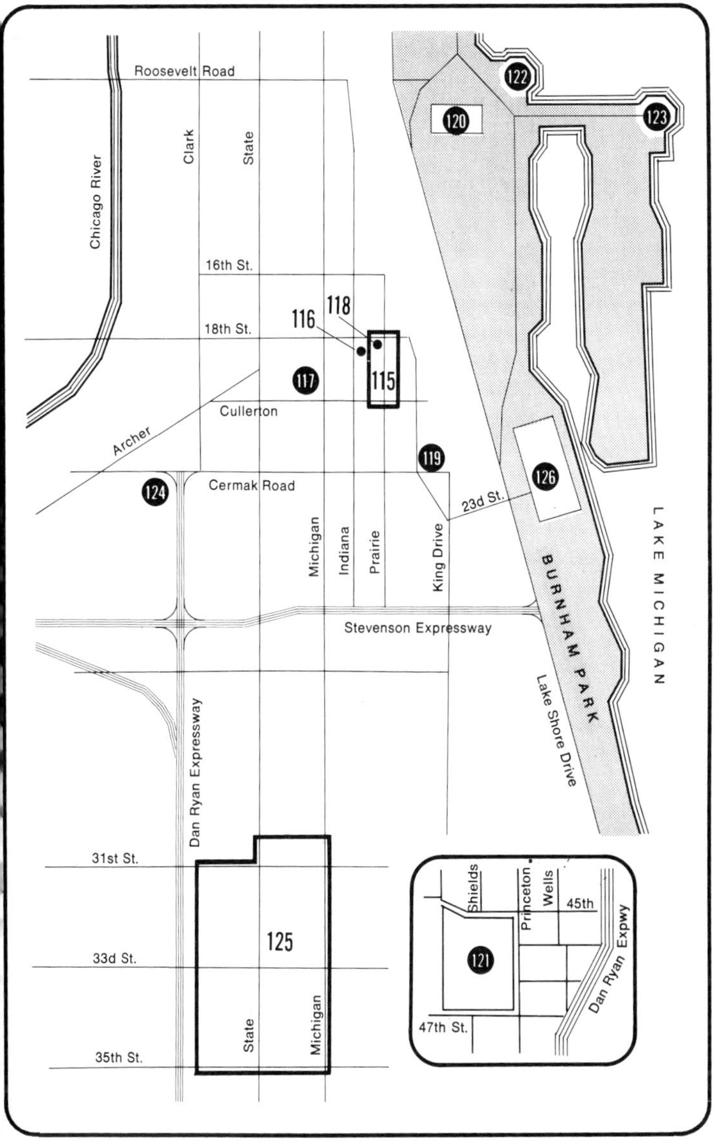

FAR NORTH AREA

127 Getty Tomb
128 Hutchinson Street District
129 Alta Vista Terrace District
130 Carl Schurz High School
131 Grover Cleveland Elementary School
132 The Emil Bach House
133 Immaculata High School
134 Krause Music Store
135 Chicago O'Hare International Airport

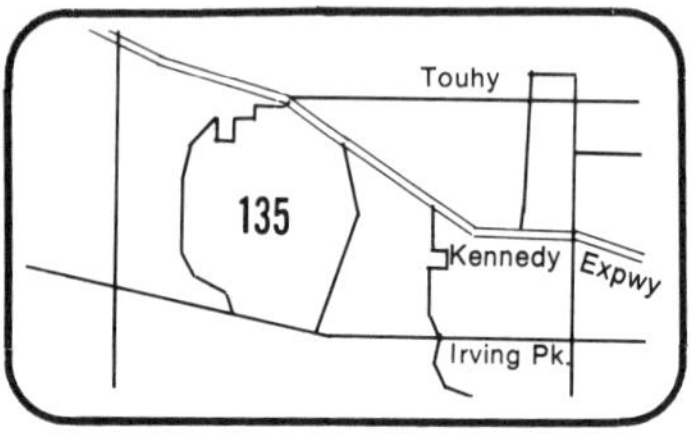

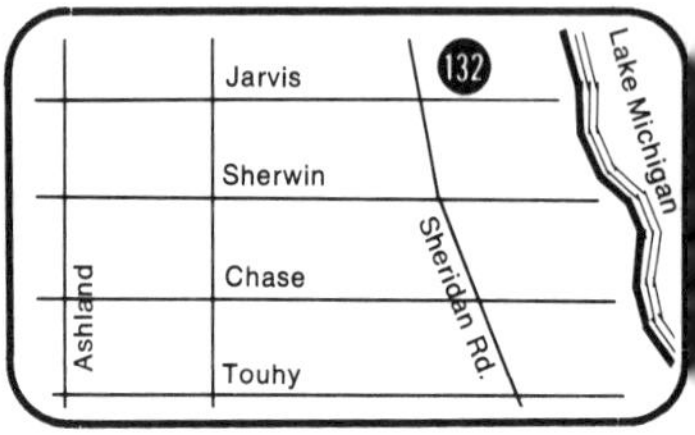

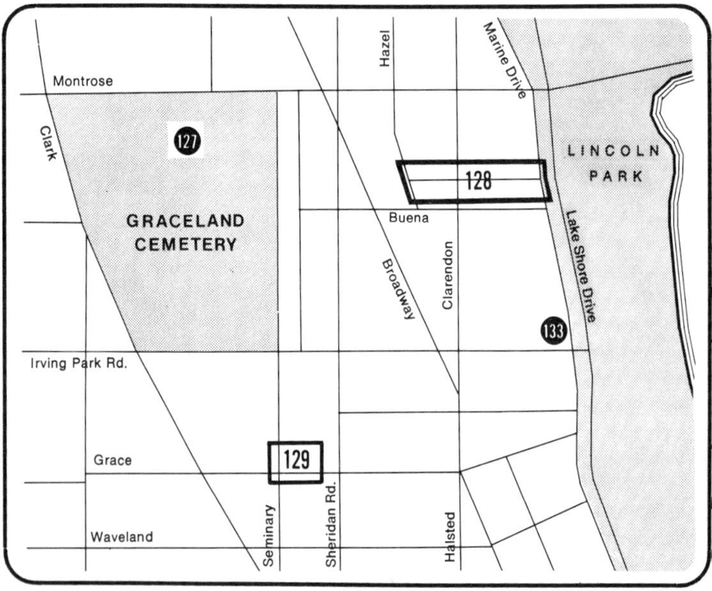

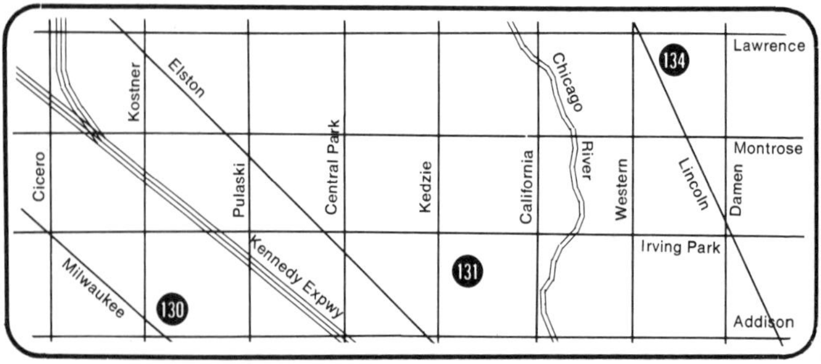

FAR SOUTH AREA

136 Kenwood District
137 South Pullman District
138 St. Gabriel's Church
139 University of Chicago Campus
140 Rockefeller Memorial Chapel
141 Museum of Science and Industry
142 Heller House
143 Magerstadt House
144 Robie House
145 South Shore Country Club
146 University Building
147 Promontory Apartments
148 Atrium Houses
149 Lutheran School of Theology

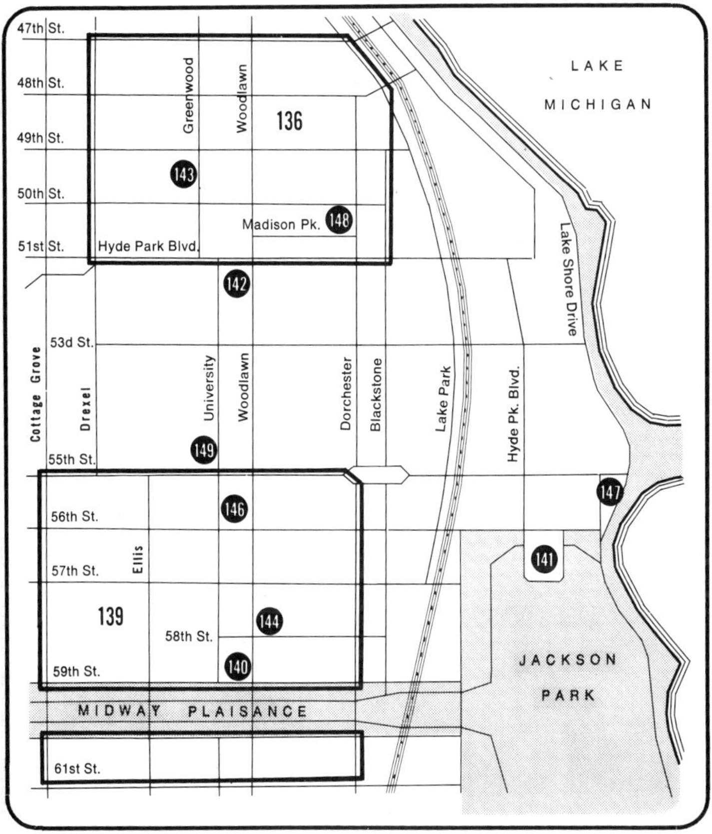

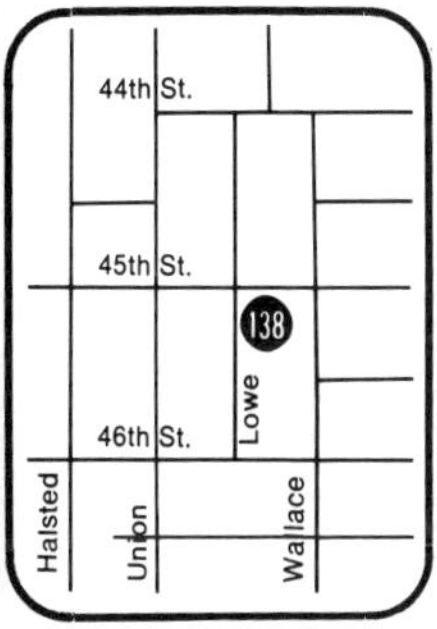

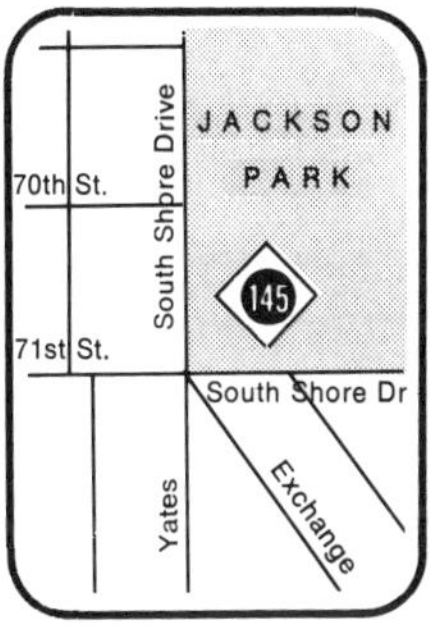

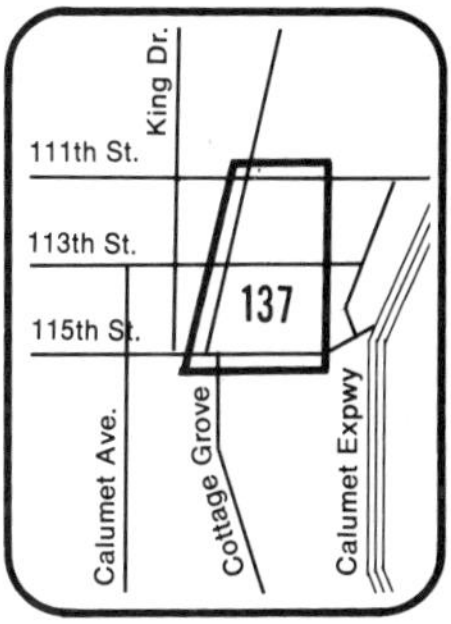

NORTH SUBURBAN AREA

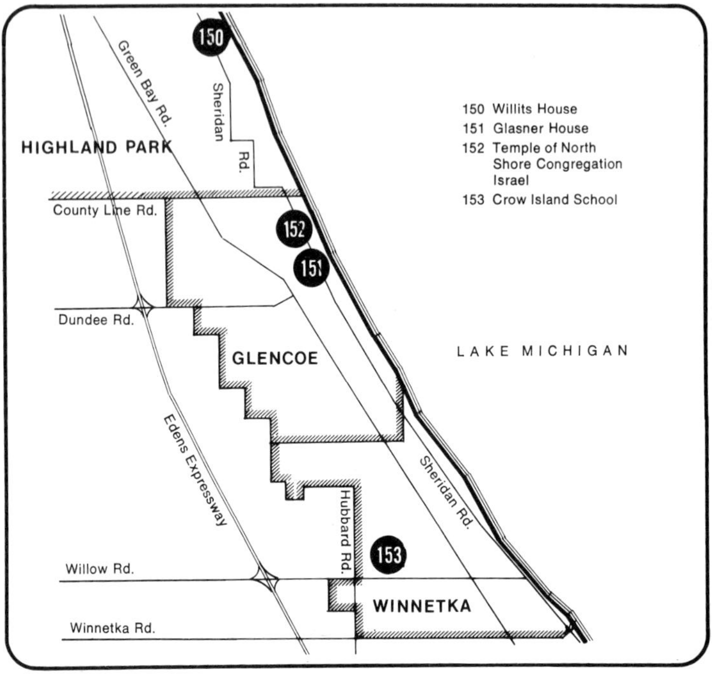

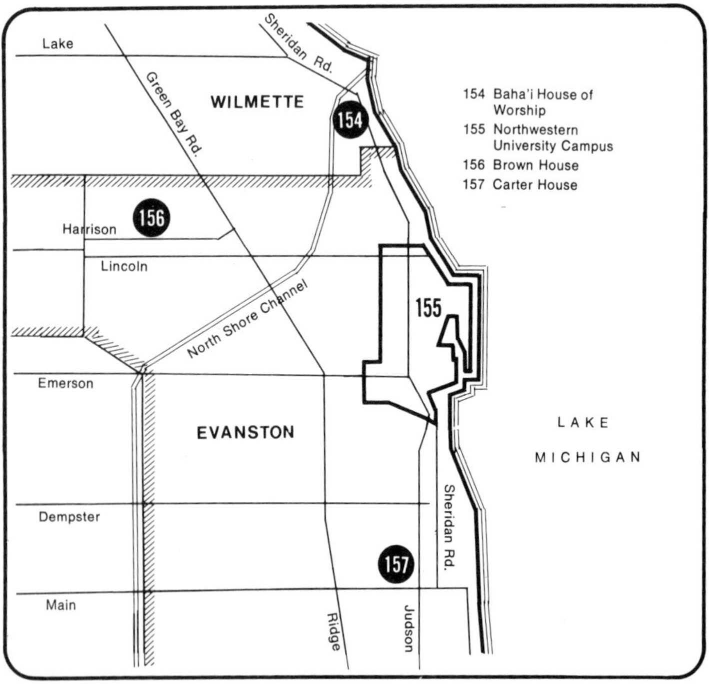

WEST SUBURBAN AREA

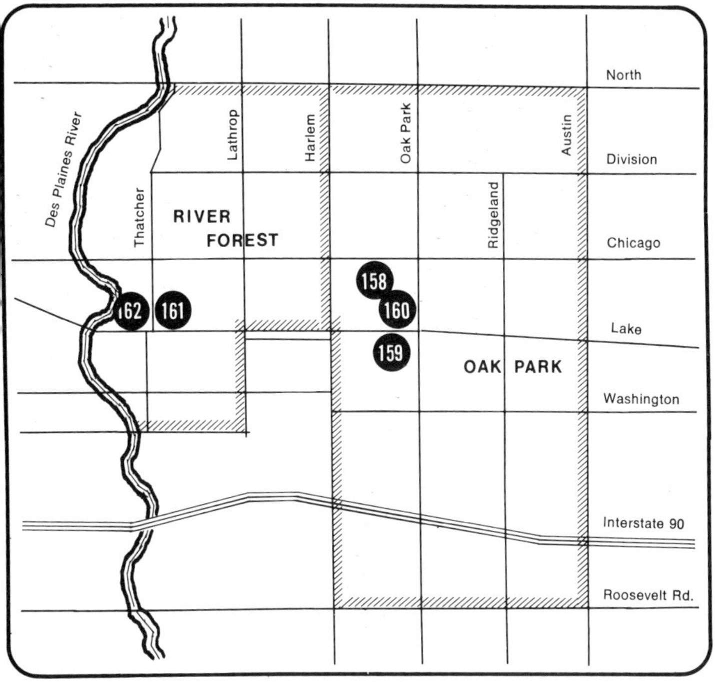

158 Frank Lloyd Wright Home and Studio
159 Unity Temple
160 Mrs. Thomas H. Gale House
161 Winslow House
162 Drummond House
163 Coonley House
164 St. Procopius Abbey

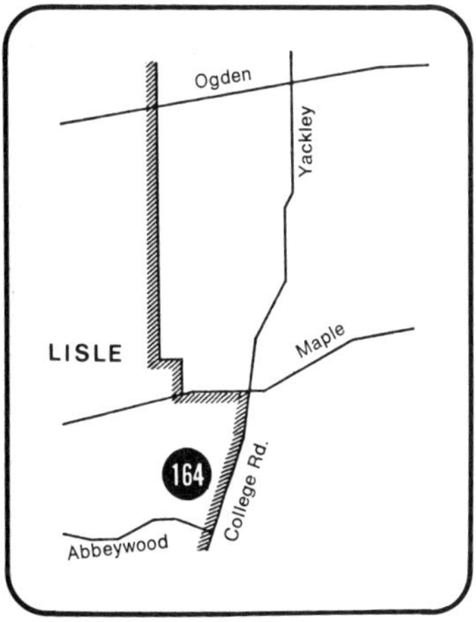

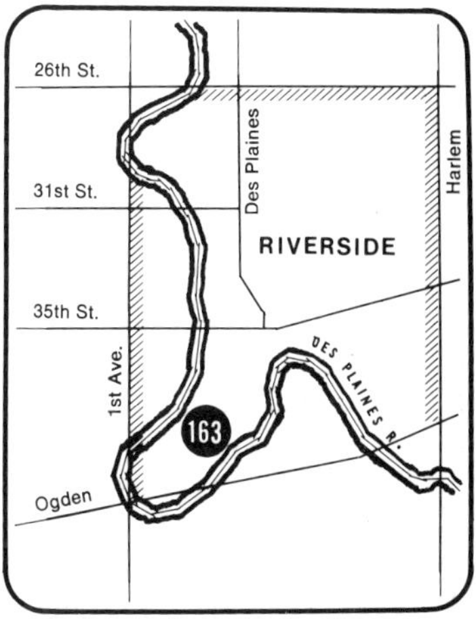

Central Area

1 Loop End Building. 1872. NR
(formerly Page Brothers)

Southeast corner of State and Lake streets.

Architect: John Mills Van Osdel.

The Lake Street facade of this building is the only cast-iron front in downtown Chicago. A cast-iron front consists of prefabricated, often finely detailed, cast-iron panels that are affixed to an otherwise traditional building which has load-bearing side walls and interior columns. Cast-iron fronts, which open a substantial surface area for windows, were common in New York beginning in 1842, and the earliest ones in Chicago were designed by Van Osdel in 1856. They lost popularity within a few years after the fire of 1871.

After State Street replaced Lake Street as Chicago's major retail thoroughfare, the State Street facade of this building, which had been a simple load-bearing masonry wall, was remodeled to become the major facade. The ground floor on Lake Street has been bricked up, the building's original cornice removed, and a sixth floor added.

2 McCarthy Building. 1872. **NR**
32 West Washington Street.

Architect: John Mills Van Osdel.

John Mills Van Osdel was the first architect to practice in Chicago, and the McCarthy Building is typical of the many commercial structures he designed in the downtown area. The windows of the top three floors are banded together horizontally under an arcade that rests on engaged columns; this is an Italianate motif that Van Osdel frequently employed. These bands of windows create a facade that was remarkably open for its day. The first two floors have been drastically altered and the original balustraded cornice replaced with an unadorned parapet. In its highly visible location at the east side of the Daley Center Plaza, the McCarthy Building provides a striking and pleasant contrast to the newer, taller buildings around it.

3 Delaware Building. 1874. **NR**
36 West Randolph Street.

Architects: Wheelock and Thomas.

The Delaware is an example of the large commercial structures built in downtown Chicago in the years immediately after the Great Fire of 1871. Its complex facade with variform window openings, deep moldings, and extensive ornament is typical of the High Victorian Italianate style which was popular at the time. The Delaware Building originally had five stories above an English basement and extended farther east along Randolph. The first two floors were of iron and glass to provide wide display windows for shops; the upper floors contained offices and did not require such wide windows. In 1889, the first two floors were remodeled, two additional floors were added, and three bays were removed from the Randolph Street facade. Inside, the original skylighted atrium lobby remains largely intact.

4 Jewelers' Building. 1882.
15–19 South Wabash Avenue.

Architects: Adler and Sullivan

The Jewelers' Building is an early work of Adler and Sullivan and is not unlike most of the three- to five-story commercial buildings that were constructed in downtown Chicago after the fire of 1871. The most distinctive features of the Jewelers' Building are its open facade and its early Sullivan ornament. The Egyptoid forms at the parapet are reminiscent of the work of Frank Furness, a Philadelphia architect for whom Sullivan worked before he came to Chicago. The ground floor has been completely remodeled, but some trace of its original ornament survives in the single pier on the north (alley) side of the structure.

5 Printing House Row. NR

South Dearborn Street between Polk and Congress streets.

After the Dearborn Street Station (No. 7) opened in 1885, many printers and publishers built plants in the immediate vicinity because of its proximity to the railroads. During the next few decades, a relatively homogeneous printing-house district developed that centered on Dearborn Street just south of the Loop. At first low loft structures were built, and later taller buildings were constructed in these blocks. The first printer to locate in the area was the Donohue and Henneberry Company, which built the structure at 711 South Dearborn in 1883. Designed by Julius Speyer, this Romanesque revival structure was efficiently organized and took advantage of its narrow lot. The heavy print-

ing presses were located in the basement, first-floor shops were rented to retail businesses, the second through fifth floors were rented to small publishers, and Donohue and Henneberry had offices on the sixth floor and used the seventh and eighth floors for book binding. An annex to the south was designed by Alfred S. Alschuler and built in 1913. The Duplicator Building, a seven-story loft structure at 530 South Dearborn built in 1886, also housed printers, as did the original Franklin Building at 523 South Dearborn, built in 1888, and the Lakeside Press Building at 731 South Plymouth Court (No. 23). A later Franklin Building was designed by George C. Nimmons and built in 1912 at 720 South Dearborn. Its facade is ornamented with colorful mosaics depicting the printing trades.

Several notable structures in the area were not built for printers. The Pontiac (No. 12), for example, was built as a speculative office building. The Terminals Building at 537 South Dearborn was built in 1892 and was one of the last works of Chicago's first architect, John Mills Van Osdel. Its oriel windows relate to those of the Morton Building across the street at 708 South Dearborn, designed by the firm of Jenney and Mundie and built in 1896 for the Morton Salt Company. The large slablike Transportation Building at 708 South Dearborn almost overwhelms the street. It was designed by Fred V. Prather and built in 1911 to house railroad offices. Its broad facade has neither horizontal nor vertical emphasis, and is consequently rather static.

After the Second World War, the printing industry changed considerably. As technology became more sophisticated, smaller printing companies were put out of business or consolidated into larger companies that could afford modern equipment; the railroads became less important as a means of transporting printed products; and auxiliary services previously performed by smaller companies were incorporated into larger printing operations. As the printing industry became less centralized, South Dearborn Street lost its identity as Printing House Row. In the late 1970s many of the structures began to be converted to residential use.

6 Fine Arts Building. 1884. CL
(Originally the Studebaker Building.)
410 South Michigan Avenue.

Architect: S. S. Beman.

This building was long notable as a focus of Chicago's artistic life because of the cultural events that took place in it and the artists who had studios there. As features of the architectural composition, the two large columns in the third and fourth stories seem incongruous in the design, perhaps needing others to keep them company. The search for variety in the shapes and groupings of the windows is carried out along the same general lines as in the Auditorium (No. 9) next door, but the result here suffers from comparison with that more masterly design.

7 Dearborn Street Station. 1885. **NR**

South Dearborn Street at West Polk Street.

Architect: Cyrus L. W. Eidlitz.

This is Chicago's only surviving late nineteenth-century passenger station. The basic composition of the Romanesque structure remains intact, although the building was greatly altered after a fire in 1922. The tall clock tower dominates the composition and terminates the vista down Dearborn Street in a visually dramatic manner matched only in downtown Chicago by the termination of LaSalle Street with the Board of Trade Building. Walls are of red pressed brick atop a base of rusticated pink granite and are ornamented by details of red terra-cotta. Prior to the 1922 fire, the building was crowned by a variety of steeply pitched roofs with dormers. The present third story of the central block is a later addition. The building has not functioned as a passenger station since 1971 and its train shed was demolished in 1976.

8 Rookery Building. 1886. **CL, NR**
209 South LaSalle Street.

Architects: Burnham and Root.

The Rookery is a transitional building, employing both masonry bearing walls in its street facades and cast-iron columns, wrought-iron spandrel beams, and steel beams elsewhere in its structure. The building wraps around an interior light court, the lower two floors of which are roofed by a skylight to create a handsome lobby space that was originally surrounded by shops and offices. This lobby was remodeled by Frank Lloyd Wright in 1905 and contains several Wrightian decorative features. The design of the exterior achieves a noteworthy combination of strength and grace. The ornament is especially interesting in its placement: in most cases it emphasizes architectural features, such as the floor lines within the larger openings, or the place a capital might be; but in other cases it seems to be addressed simply and courteously to the spectator's enjoyment. The vigorous contrast of columns and heavy stonework is more effective and more unified than in the Fine Arts Building (No. 6). This contrast, as well as the combination of massive walls and large windows and the degree of emphasis at the corners, top, and center of the facade, all help to establish the building's strong presence. John Root held that the virtues of architecture were similar to the traits of civilized people, and the Rookery can well be viewed in this way. It stands there like a stronghearted and cheerful person, forceful, yet friendly.

9 **Auditorium Building. 1889. CL, NR**
South Michigan Avenue and Congress Street (NW corner).

Architects: Adler and Sullivan.

The Auditorium was Adler and Sullivan's first major commission, and its design and construction demonstrated Sullivan's developing genius and Adler's engineering skills. A complex structure meant to incorporate a grand theater, a hotel, and an office building presented complex engineering problems which Adler successfully tackled. The immense weight of the load-bearing granite and limestone walls was unevenly distributed (being much greater beneath the tower on Congress Street), and Adler devised an ingenious foundation system to equalize settlement of the structure. Nevertheless, substantial settlement occurred demonstrating the need for deep foundations under such heavy buildings. Adler also devised a complex system of interior iron framing that, among other things, carried the hotel kitchen and dining hall on trusses above the stage and auditorium space. For the theater, Adler devised a hydraulically operated stage and an early system of air conditioning. The acoustics of the theater are superb, another product of Adler's genius. Sullivan designed a straightforward facade whose powerful rhythm of simple geometric forms is based on H. H. Richardson's design of the Marshall Field Wholesale Store (which stood until 1930 at Adams and Wells). On the interior, especially in the theater, Sullivan's original ornament contributes to the grandeur of this monumental civic structure. The Auditorium flourished until the 1930s. After a period of decline, it was purchased in 1946 by Roosevelt University. The theater itself remained in disrepair until the 1960s, when the Auditorium Theater Council undertook its restoration, reopening it in 1968.

10 Manhattan Building. 1890. **CL, NR**
431 South Dearborn Street.

Architect: William LeBaron Jenney.

The structural advances that led to the development of the Chicago School contributed to the emergence of a dichotomy between the role of architect and that of engineer. Jenney was primarily an engineer, and the Manhattan Building represents an important engineering accomplishment. This building and Burnham and Root's Rand McNally Building (now demolished) were the first tall office buildings to use skeleton construction throughout. Even the party walls were carried by the steel frame, in this case on beams cantilevered out, that is, extending beyond their supporting columns. The building thus displays Jenney's interest in structural matters and his inventiveness in using the new structural material, either iron or steel. The design of the Manhattan, however, is not particularly impressive. The various materials and the different shapes of the bay windows, for instance, produce an effect of disunity.

11 Monadnock Building. 1891. **CL, NR**
53 West Jackson Boulevard.

Architects: Burnham and Root; south half: Holabird and Roche (1893).

The Monadnock is the tallest wall-bearing structure in Chicago. To support the weight of its sixteen stories, the walls are six feet thick at the base; this extreme thickness demonstrated that it was not feasible to build any higher using traditional masonry construction. The Monadnock is modern in its simplicity; no traces of applied ornamentation are found in its design. Visual interest is created by gently projecting bays that alternate and contrast with deeply set windows. The inward curve of the walls above the first story is reversed at the top with the walls "chamfered" off. A later addition to the south by Holabird and Roche employs skeleton construction and continues the Monadnock's pattern of bays, creating a strong rhythm along the Dearborn Street facade.

12 Pontiac Building. 1891. **NR**
542 South Dearborn Street.

Architects: Holabird and Roche.

The Pontiac is the oldest surviving building designed by Holabird and Roche. Its simply treated brick walls and gently projecting oriels are reminiscent of Burnham and Root's Monadnock Building of the same year. In the Pontiac, however, the exterior walls do not support the building but rather form a taut skin that sheathes the skeleton frame. The frame is less forcefully expressed here than in other Holabird and Roche facades. Here, the wide oriels of the east and west facades span two structural bays; consequently, at the center of each of these oriels is a vertical member of the frame that is not expressed on the exterior. Nevertheless, the Pontiac was a step toward the clarity of expression that Holabird and Roche achieved in their 1895 Marquette Building and subsequent designs.

PONTIAC CAFETERIA — GRILL
PONTIAC CAFETERIA — GRILL
542

13 Second Leiter Building. 1891. NR
(now Sears, Roebuck and Company.)
State and Van Buren streets (SE corner).

Architects: Jenney and Mundie.

This building is an example of the "commercial style" for which Chicago was famous. The piers are narrow enough to suggest the metal frame within them, as do the slender piers and high ceilings of the interior. Ornament is sparse, economy is suggested, and the general effect is simple and direct.

14 Art Institute of Chicago. 1892.
Michigan Avenue at Adams Street.

Architects: Shepley, Rutan and Coolidge (1892); for McKinlock Court: Coolidge and Hodgson (1924); for North Wing: Holabird and Root (1956); for Morton Wing: Shaw, Metz and Associates (1962); for East Wing: Skidmore, Owings and Merrill (1976) (Walter A. Netsch, partner in charge); reconstruction of Stock Exchange Trading Room: Vinci/Kenny (1977).

Chief home of the visual arts in Chicago, the building, like many museums of its time, was inspired by the architectural tradition of the Renaissance as taught in the Ecole des Beaux-Arts in Paris, and is thus frankly traditional in character. The McKinlock Court, built in 1924 in the eastern enlargement, Coolidge and Hodgson architects, is a pleasant

oasis of classicism. Here lunch is served in the open air in summer. The classical arcades of the court are not quite overwhelmed by the rout of sea creatures in the fountain by Carl Milles. (This fountain, set up in 1931, is a duplicate of one in Lidingo, Sweden.)

An east wing contains 216,500 square feet facing Columbus Drive: entry, dining facilities, auditorium, galleries around McKinlock Court, and a new facility for the school of art. The high-ceilinged trading room of Adler and Sullivan's Stock Exchange Building (demolished in 1972) was incorporated in the new construction, and the entry arch of the old building was reerected in a new garden. Near the Columbus Drive entrance stands Isamu Noguchi's bicentennial fountain sculpture.

15 54 West Hubbard Street. 1892.

Architect: Otto H. Matz.

This Romanesque structure was built as the Criminal Court. The use of this style for courthouses became popular as a result of H. H. Richardson's Allegheny County Courthouse and Jail in Pittsburgh, Pennsylvania, which was designed in 1884. Although the 54 West Hubbard building is less inspired than many of the Romanesque courthouses built in the late 1880s and early 1890s, it is nevertheless handsome. Matz was an early Chicago architect who served for a period as architect for the Chicago public schools.

16 Congress Hotel. 1893.
504 South Michigan.

Architects: Clinton J. Warren; Holabird and Roche (1902, 1907).

The architects of the Chicago School created the modern hotel and apartment building as well as the office block, and the Congress is the best and largest of the multiple-dwelling structures. The vertical banks of projecting oriel windows, a distinguishing feature of many Chicago hotels and office buildings, allow the maximum admission of light, at the same time imparting to the long street elevations a vigorous sense of rhythmic movement. The broad openings of the base and the light screenlike walls clearly suggest a thin curtain drawn over the columns and girders of the steel frame. The original rough-faced granite blocks of the first story and the shape of the paired windows in the upper three stories indicate that Warren was deliberately trying to harmonize the initial block of the hotel with the Auditorium Building (No. 9) immediately to the north.

17 Marshall Field and Company Store. NR
1893, 1902, 1906, 1907.

Block bounded by Wabash Avenue and State Street, and Washington and Randolph streets.

Architects: D. H. Burnham and Company.

This enormous structure houses one of the world's best-known department stores. The earliest section of the present store is the heavily rusticated Renaissance palazzo-like edifice at the northwest corner of Wabash and Washington. This was built in 1893 as an annex to an 1879 structure occupied by Field's at the northeast corner of State and Washington. The north half of the State Street front was next completed, and then the north half of the Wabash Avenue front. The original 1879 building was demolished and replaced by the present south half of the State Street front in 1907. The design of the three later sections is commercial in function, classical in inspiration. It consists of a three-story base,

a seven-story central section topped by an entablature, and a two-story columned top with a classical cornice. The main entrance on State Street has a high portico with four Ionic columns of Carrara marble resting on granite bases and topped by an entablature and a carved marble balustrade. Perhaps the most familiar exterior features are the elaborate clocks at the corners of the State Street facade. On the interior, a light court in the southwest section features a dome designed by Louis Comfort Tiffany. The Field Store is the prototype of other large urban department stores that Burnham designed for Selfridge's in London (1906; Selfridge was a former Field partner); Gimble's in New York (1909); Wanamaker's in Philadelphia (1909); the May Company in Cleveland (1912); and Filene's in Boston (1912).

18 Old Colony Building. 1894. **CL, NR**
407 South Dearborn Street.

Architects: Holabird and Roche.

The Old Colony is the last remaining downtown building with rounded projecting corner bays, a device often employed by Holabird and Roche and other architects to create highly desirable corner spaces on the interior and an interesting silhouette on the exterior. Note that continuous vertical piers along Dearborn Street balance the breadth of that facade, while continuous horizontal spandrels along Van Buren Street emphasize the width of the narrow facade. The Old Colony was the first structure to employ a system of portal arches to brace it against wind loads, an innovative solution to a basic problem of tall skeleton-framed buildings. Portal bracing had long been employed in bridge construction and had been introduced into the construction of skyscrapers, although not in the arched form used here, in the early 1890s.

19 Marquette Building. 1894. **CL, NR**
140 South Dearborn Street.

Architects: Holabird and Roche.

In the Marquette, Holabird and Roche gave forceful aesthetic expression to the skeleton frame and developed the basic pattern that would characterize their work for the next thirty years. This pattern consists of strong, continuous projecting piers and less forceful, recessed spandrels framing wide Chicago windows to create a cellular facade that expresses the geometry of the supporting frame. The treatment of the top and bottom follows Sullivan's idea of setting these stories off from the others. The building was originally topped by a cornice which was later removed and replaced by the present unsightly top floor. The bay at the western end of the Adams Street facade is also a later addition. Brilliant mosaics in the lobby and bronze reliefs above the entrance depict incidents in the life of Père Marquette, an early explorer of this area. After a period when its existence was threatened by developers, the Marquette underwent extensive renovation in the late 1970s.

20 Reliance Building. 1895. **CL, NR**
36 North State Street.

Architects: D. H. Burnham and Company.

The Reliance was a remarkably advanced structure for its time. Once the skeletal frame had freed the exterior walls from their function, buildings could be sheathed almost entirely in glass. No building of its day came closer to this than the Reliance. Slender piers and mullions and narrow spandrels, all of

cream-colored terra-cotta (darkened now after years of neglect), and broad windows contribute to the openness of the facade. The strength and convenience of steel construction were shown in the piecemeal manner in which the building was constructed. In 1890 John Root designed a sixteen-story building for this site, but only the foundations and first story were built at that time. These were "slipped under" the upper stories of a four-story, heavy masonry building already there, these upper stories continuing in use during construction. In 1894 the older stories were "knocked off" and the present building carried on up. The designer in charge in 1894–95 was Charles Atwood of D. H. Burnham and Company, who apparently redesigned the exteriors. It was at this time that the present terra-cotta sheathing was designed.

21 Fisher Building. 1896. **CL, NR**
343 South Dearborn Street.

Architects: D. H. Burnham and Company.

This is an early example of the application of Gothic style to the skyscraper, an ornamental scheme that would become popular briefly during the 1920s. The detail is consistently Gothic in inspiration, and the corner piers are even given a Gothic form with engaged colonnettes (or moldings). One may note the emphasis on height which this accomplishes, aided here by the verticals of the projecting bays. The design achieves a notable openness and lightness, hardly inferior to the Reliance Building, and thus vigorously expresses the steel frame despite the presence of the historical detail.

22 Chicago Public Library Cultural Center. 1897. CL, NR

78 East Washington Street.

Architects: Shepley, Rutan and Coolidge (1897); Architects for restoration: Holabird and Root (1977).

From its completion in 1897 until 1974, the structure now known as the Chicago Public Library Cultural Center housed the central operations of the Chicago Public Library. By the late 1960s it had become evident that the central library collections and the functions of the library system had outgrown the building. The library's board of directors studied the problem and decided to renovate the building as a popular library and a center for the library's cultural activities, with the idea of constructing a new building to house most of the library's collection.

The building entrances are on the north and south sides, each serving a different area of the building. The exterior design and elements of the interior are derived from Italian Renaissance precedents. Many walls are wainscoted with wood or marble; some are paneled for their entire height in marble. The floors are covered with mosaic tile. The Washington Street portion contains a grand staircase of white Carrara marble. The balustrades are inlaid with intricate mosaics designed in the Tiffany style and composed of marble and glass around medallions of dark green Irish marble.

The third floor adjoining the grand staircase is a civic reception center which houses an illuminated stained-glass Tiffany dome. The design of the fourth floor, where the Exhibition Hall is located, is based on several Italian Renaissance palaces. The Randolph Street entrance is more subdued and a quiet staircase leads to the second floor Grand Army of the Republic Memorial Hall and small theater—both refurbished while retaining the original Tiffany stained-glass dome and remarkably well-preserved wall fixtures. An addition has been built along Garland Court, filling in the U-shape and enabling people to cross from the north to the south side on all floors which had not previously been possible. The addition encloses a garden court.

23 731 South Plymouth Building. 1897. NR
(Originally the Lakeside Press Building.)
731 South Plymouth Court.

Architect: Howard VanDoren Shaw.

This vigorous design is of generally traditional character, but freely treated so that it seems original rather than imitative. The facade gains interest from the way the arches over some of the openings are played off against the flat heads, or lintels, of others and the greater openness of the upper stories against the greater solidness of the lower two. The spandrels (horizontal strips of wall at the floor levels) in the upper stories, and the window glass throughout, are set well back from the surfaces of the piers to show their mass, which contributes greatly to the vigor and strength of the whole design. The centerpiece, around the doors, is interesting in its modifications of classical motifs. The coat-of-arms, with its Indian head and the representation of Fort Dearborn in relief, and the medallions refer to series of books published by the Lakeside Press.

24 Gage Building. 1898. NR

18 South Michigan Avenue.

Architects: Holabird and Roche; Louis H. Sullivan.

Only the facade of this building was designed by Sullivan. Note the fine relations established among piers, windows, and wall surfaces; the excellence of proportions throughout; and the imaginative use of original ornament. Sometimes Sullivan's ornament seems plastered on at spots, rather than integrated with a building, and the two bursts of ornament at the tops of the piers suggest as much in this instance. However, the architect designed only an eight-story facade; the other four stories were added in 1902. Comparison of photographs taken before and after suggests that this ornament was perhaps "held in" better in the smaller facade. There was also a band of rich, though more delicate, ornament along the top of the first story, which probably helped. The two buildings to the south, 30 and 24 South Michigan, were done entirely by Holabird and Roche. Their facades form an interesting contrast with that of the Gage Building. The basic design is the same, but they do not have the refinement and elegance of proportion and accent to be found in the Gage. In their avoidance of ornament they seem to look to the future more directly than does Sullivan's design.

25 Carson Pirie Scott and Company Store. CL, NR
1899, 1903–4.
(Originally the Schlesinger and Mayer Store.)
State and Madison streets (SE corner).

Architect: Louis H. Sullivan.

The easternmost section of three bays on Madison Street was built first, and the main section, extending around the corner and with seven bays on State Street, several years later. (The third section was done by D. H. Burnham and Company in 1906, and the southernmost by Holabird and Root in 1960–61.) The wide windows and narrow piers express the steel frame, but the details suggest the sensitive designer above all. The fine proportions of the window openings, the firm emphasis in the moldings around them, the accent given by the line of delicate ornament on the horizontal wall sections, all contribute to a perfection of design rarely to be found. The rich ornament of the first and second floors has been criticized as too ornate for a commercial building. One should note, however, that Sullivan held that the display windows were like pictures and

deserved rich frames, and his prophetic power is seen in this, if one compares old photographs showing the stodgy displays of the time with window-dressers' art of today. The ornament has been returned to its original reddish-green color after years of being painted gray. Sullivan intended the ornament to resemble oxidized bronze, an effect achieved by applying a coat of brownish-red paint and then applying a layer of deep green paint in such a way that the undercoat of red shows through in places. Other features of the original design have also been restored. A ceiling that had been added later was removed from the rotunda entrance, revealing the original column capitals. The glass panels on the outside and inside of the rotunda have been opened up so that natural light is admitted to the store. Chicago architect John Vinci was responsible for the renovation.

As in many of the older buildings, the original projection, or cornice, at the top has been replaced by a bald parapet. The large festoons of ornament which were originally set outside the piers between the first and second floors have also been removed. (One wonders whether they could ever have seemed very closely related to the wall, rather than "hung on" it.) They contained the initials "SM" for the owners. The architect's initials "LHS" can still be seen in some of the ornament, perhaps slipped in by George G. Elmslie, who, as Sullivan's chief designer, carried out much of the ornamental design.

Carson Pirie Scott and Company Store

26 Wieboldt's Annex. 1900, 1905.
(Originally Mandel Brothers Annex.)

Northwest corner of Wabash Avenue and Madison Street.

Architects: Holabird and Roche.

This distinguished building compares favorably with Sullivan's masterpiece, the Carson Pirie Scott Store (No. 25). Wide window bays and narrow piers contribute to the openness of the facade, and continuous projecting bands of ornament at the sill level of the windows emphasize the strong horizontality. The lower eight floors were built first, and the top three were added five years later.

27 McClurg Building. 1900. NR

218 South Wabash Avenue.

Architects: Holabird and Roche.

The light and open character of the facade is remarkable. Compare the relative emphasis on the horizontal versus the vertical and on openness versus solidity in the treatment of the wall of this building and those of the Marquette Building (No. 19) and the Carson Pirie Scott Store (No. 25). The three buildings also offer interesting comparisons of the treatment of the "Chicago window," that is, a window in which a fixed center light is flanked by movable sashes at the sides.

28 Chapin and Gore Building. 1904.
(Later the Nepeennauk Building, now the 63 East Adams Building.)
63 East Adams Street.

Architect: Richard E. Schmidt.

There is an originality almost mannerist here, as in the split window-framing panels on the second floor, contrasting with the beautifully simple piers above. These piers originally flowered at the top in "upside-down capitals," as they were called when first seen, which unfortunately have been removed. Also the original cornice has been replaced with a parapet, and this, with the absence of the original capitals, makes the upper part of the building incongruously bare in relation to the lower part.

29 Railway Exchange Building. 1904.

80 East Jackson Boulevard.

Architects: D. H. Burnham and Company.

The Railway Exchange was built to house the offices of several railroads at a time when Chicago was the rail center of the country. Burnham was not only the architect, but was also a major investor in the building and maintained his offices there for several years. The facade has an extremely delicate quality: its considerable glass area is articulated by gleaming white terra-cotta molded into delicate ornament. The oriels project very slightly, creating a gentle rhythm along both street facades. The building is square in plan and has a central light well, the lower floors of which form a spacious lobby. This lobby originally had a transparent skylight to admit natural light, but it was later tarred over to prevent leakage.

30 Chicago Building. 1904. **NR**
7 West Madison Street.

Architects: Holabird and Roche.

The Chicago Building is another of the high-quality designs produced by the prolific firm of Holabird and Roche. Continuous vertical piers emphasize the height of the narrow State Street facade. This verticality is repeated in the projecting bays along Madison Street that alternate with wide windows to create a rhythm that carries the longer facade. The corner piers are emphasized as in the firm's earlier Marquette Building. The top and bottom floors are set off from the intervening floors, also recalling the design of the Marquette. Note how the Chicago Building contrasts with its neighbor across the street, the Carson Pirie Scott Store. The tall vertical mass of the Chicago Building contrasts with the horizontality of the Carson store; the deeply modeled facade of the Chicago Building with its projecting piers and bays and its recessed windows contrasts with the flat surface of the Carson facade. The Chicago Building is one of the few downtown structures that has its original cornice intact, although today the building's original reddish-brown brick and terra-cotta sheathing is blackened by grime.

31 Orchestra Hall. 1905. NR

220 South Michigan Avenue.

Architect: D. H. Burnham and Company; ninth-floor addition by Howard Van Doren Shaw (completed 1908); interior renovation by Harry Weese and Associates (completed 1966).

This neo-Georgian building reflects D. H. Burnham's growing interest in revival styles following the World's Columbian Exposition in 1893. The symmetrical facade (ignoring the more simply treated southernmost bay) is of red brick complemented by limestone quoins, lintels, and other decorative features characteristic of the Georgian revival style. The tall windows of the second floor capped by Georgian fanlights reflect a high-ceilinged ballroom used for receptions and chamber concerts. The facade is topped by a classical cornice and a balustrade that hides a later ninth-floor addition. The auditorium space where the orchestra performs is at the west of the building and is four stories high. Above the fourth floor, the building is only one office space deep, creating a light court at the rear of the structure.

Orchestra Hall has been the home of the Chicago Symphony Orchestra for over seventy years. Organized by Theodore Thomas in 1891, the orchestra initially performed in Adler and Sullivan's Auditorium Theater. Thomas frequently complained that the Auditorium was too large and even threatened to quit as conductor before the Orchestral Association agreed to build a smaller hall. Burnham, as a trustee of the Orchestral Association, donated his design services. Within a few weeks after the orchestra first performed in the hall in December 1904, Thomas died. Burnham and others urged that the hall be named after the orchestra's founder and first conductor, so that the formal name of the building, "Theodore Thomas Orchestra Hall," is carved in stone above the entrance.

BACH
MOZART
BEETHOVEN
SCHUBERT
WAGNER

32 Blackstone Hotel. 1909.
South Michigan Avenue at East Balbo Avenue.

Architects: Marshall and Fox.

At the end of the first decade of the twentieth century, architects were busy applying historical ornament to tall commercial buildings, and the principles of the Chicago School had largely been eclipsed. The Blackstone Hotel is one of the better revival-style buildings produced in Chicago at this time. Here, forms and details of the French Second Empire style have been applied to the twenty-two-story hotel. The same architects also designed the small Blackstone Theater to the west. Built in 1911, the theater is based on French Renaissance precedents.

33 Brooks Building. 1910.

223 West Jackson Boulevard.

Architects: Holabird and Roche.

A late work of the Chicago School, the Brooks Building has a spectacularly open facade that directly reflects the skeleton frame. A strong vertical emphasis is created by the division of each pier into a cluster of long narrow columns and by the vertical moldings within each horizontal spandrel. The piers terminate in a burst of ornament reminiscent of that at the tops of the piers of the Gage Building (No. 24), which Louis Sullivan designed in collaboration with Holabird and Roche in 1898—although here perhaps the ornament is better integrated with the rest of the facade. Note the variation of the "Chicago window"; here a wide movable sash replaces the typical central stationary pane of glass.

Brooks Building

34 Chicago and Northwestern Station. 1911.
Madison Street between Canal and Clinton streets.

Architects: Frost and Granger.

This was the earlier of two mammoth railroad stations (see also Union Station, No. 43) built at the time that rail traffic reached its peak in Chicago. Both represent major achievements in planning for the efficient handling of the tremendous volume of rail traffic anticipated at that time. An earlier Chicago and Northwestern Station designed by W. W. Boyington was completed in 1881 at Wells and Kinzie streets. Within twenty-five years, rail traffic had increased so phenomenally that a much larger station was required. Frost and Granger were commissioned to design the new station in 1906, construction began in 1908, and the station opened in 1911. The station is so large and well planned that it has been estimated that it could easily accommodate 500 trains and 250,000 passengers per day

although traffic has seldom been more than half that great.

The headhouse, as the entrance building of a railroad terminal is called, is a monumental Renaissance-style masonry structure that fronts on Madison Street. A central entrance portico with six enormous granite columns extends the full height of the facade. The ground floor, now largely closed, contained various subsidiary facilities. The main waiting room is on the second floor, as are ticket offices, restaurants, the concourse, platforms, and tracks. The immense waiting room is the major interior space and is expressed on the exterior by the barrel vault that projects above the roof line. This room is 202 feet long, 102 feet wide, and 84 feet high at the top of its vaulted ceiling. Beyond the main waiting room is the train shed that projects 894 feet beyond the headhouse at its farthest point. Eight platforms and sixteen tracks are housed under a series of low concrete vaults supported by steel ribs resting on columns.

Never before had a station this enormous and complex been built in Chicago, and its construction demonstrated the feasibility of consolidating the scattered downtown railroad stations into one enormous union station. That was attempted a few years later when planning for Union Station began.

35 City Hall—County Building. 1911.
LaSalle, Randolph, Clark, and Washington streets.

Architects: Holabird and Roche.

This colossal monolithic neoclassical structure covers an entire city block. When viewed from the Daley Center Plaza to the east, it makes a most impressive backdrop to this great downtown open space. Actually, the structure is composed of two buildings linked by passageways at various levels. The original design called for a domed center which was never constructed for reasons of cost. The building is twelve stories high, with two basements. The dimensions are 337 feet long on LaSalle and Clark streets by 214 feet wide on Washington and Randolph Streets. The exterior is of Bedford limestone throughout, with the exception of a granite base on LaSalle. The City Council Chamber is on the second floor (LaSalle Street) and the Mayor's office and County Board offices are on the fifth. The spacious lobbies on the first floor with their vaulted ceilings covered with mosaics provide an impressive entry to this monumental civic building.

36 **Dwight Building. 1911.**

626 South Clark Street.

Architects: Schmidt, Garden and Martin.

This building shows the application of the general principles of design seen in the Montgomery Ward Warehouse (No. 89) to an office building. Similar framing strips can be seen on the horizontals but here are limited to the upper edge of these members. Hardly interrupting the upward movement of the wall, these accents distinguish the sills from the heads of the windows and emphasize the agreeable horizontal proportions of the windows themselves.

37 City of Chicago Central Office Building. 1913. (Originally Reid, Murdoch and Company.) **CL, NR**

320 North Clark Street.

Architect: George C. Nimmons.

This structure is typical of a number of buildings designed by Nimmons for commercial or manufacturing use. It is simple and straightforward, although with some traditional feeling, as in the massiveness emphasized at points here. The brick is used very effectively for its texture and pattern, finely set off by terra-cotta accents. The building is now well maintained and gives a good idea of the original, although it has been remodeled, one bay having been removed from its west side when LaSalle Street was widened.

38 Chicago Theater. 1921.
175 North State Street.

Architects: C. W. and George L. Rapp.

Designed by a firm noted for its theaters, the Chicago is an early example of the lavish movie palaces of the 1920s where fantasy and illusion were not restricted to the screen but extended to the architectural surroundings as well. The State Street facade, partially obscured by a later marquee and six-story vertical sign, is organized on a triumphal arch motif; the off-white terra-cotta sheathing is molded into neobaroque ornamental forms. The interior follows the precedent of French Second Empire style designs which revived baroque forms to create an effect of overwhelming grandeur. Although the inner lobby has unfortunately been remodeled, most of the original ornament remains intact.

39 Wrigley Building. 1921, 1924.
North Michigan Avenue at the River (north bank).

Architects: Graham, Anderson, Probst and White.

The Wrigley Building is the earliest of the celebrated skyscraper group at Michigan and the river (see also Nos. 40, 42, and 45). The terra-cotta sheathing of the frame carries rather commonplace ornament derived from Renaissance designs, and the building achieved fame through traits other than architectural merit. It was floodlit from the beginning, and because of the almost white terra-cotta, furnished visitors of the 1920s with a dazzling sight. Behind the thin screen that unites the main building and its annex is a handsome little plaza with planting and fountain nicely scaled to the narrow area.

40 Stone Container Building. 1923.
(Originally London Guarantee Building.)
360 North Michigan Avenue.

Architect: Alfred S. Alschuler.

Because of its irregular site where Wacker Drive curves to meet Michigan Avenue, this twenty-one-story building has a vaguely trapezoidal plan. The east facade follows the regular north-side axis of Michigan Avenue and is broken above the fifth floor by a deep light court, the west facade angles away to follow Wacker Drive, and the north side is broken to create a concave facade oriented toward the river. The five-story base and three-story top display ornamental forms derived from classical precedents, while the central floors exhibit the vertical bands of windows and strong, continuous piers common to skyscrapers of the late 1920s. Four Corinthian columns flank a central arched entrance and support a classical entablature, forming a grand entrance that dominates the base. A classical colonnade marks the top three stories. The cornice is topped by a balustrade, and the entire composition is crowned by an elaborate, round, domed pavilion supported by columns.

41 Continental Illinois National Bank and Trust Company Building. 1924.

231 South LaSalle Street.

Architects: Graham, Anderson, Probst and White.

Built as the Illinois Merchants Bank, this nineteen-story building expresses both the dignity and grandeur considered appropriate to a banking establishment of the time. With the exception of the tall Ionic columns at the entrance, the facade is simply treated and unadorned. Inside, the enormous banking floor, with its tall columns and high coffered ceiling is not only a monument to the world of finance but is also one of the grandest interior spaces in the city.

42 Tribune Tower. 1925.
North Michigan Avenue at the River (north bank).

Architects: Hood and Howells.

Familiar to the general public as the home of the *Chicago Tribune,* the Tribune Tower is known among architects and students of architecture as the winning design in an international competition held by the newspaper in 1922. Although this Gothic revival design won first place, the wide discussion of the award led to general agreement that the modern office building, or skyscraper, should be designed in a modern style. The discussion has obscured some of the virtues which, modern or not, this building has, such as the active and picturesque silhouette and the interesting treatment of the wall, with vertical sections of different widths. The simpler brick structure just east of and joined to the Tower was built as a separate building, the Tribune Plant, and designed by architect Jarvis Hunt. (Its south side was surfaced with stone in 1965.)

43 Union Station. 1925.
Canal Street between Adams Street and Jackson Boulevard.

Architects: Graham, Burnham and Company (1913–17); Graham, Anderson, Probst and White (after 1917).

The Union Station complex originally consisted of two separate structures on either side of Canal Street, connected below grade by a broad vaulted tunnel. The larger structure is the eight-story headhouse that still stands on the west side of Canal Street. Early plans for the complex incorporated the headhouse into a twenty-story office building, and the existing foundations are sufficient to support such a structure. Above its colonnaded base, the headhouse as built has a simple office-block facade. Only the high colonnade and wide entrances at the centers of the north and south facades mark it as a train station. Inside the headhouse, stairs lead down into the main waiting room. This monumental space is 112 feet high to the top of its vaulted skylight, and

is surrounded by enormous Corinthian columns that contribute to its grand scale. Two free-standing columns supporting allegorical figures of Day and Night mark the entrance to the below-grade passageway that originally led to the concourse building on the east side of Canal.

The concourse building was a classically styled, pedimented structure that was demolished in 1969 and replaced by an office building. This eastern building contained the vast passenger concourse that was the most impressive space in the station complex. Modeled on the concourse of New York's Pennsylvania Station (now also demolished), the space was roofed by three parallel glass and tile vaults carried on steel arch ribs which were supported by steel lattice columns. At the north and south sides of the passenger concourse were low train concourses that ended in train platforms and tracks.

The station serves two separate sets of tracks, ten extending to the north and fourteen to the south. It has been estimated that the station can easily accommodate a total of 720 trains and 400.000 passengers per day, although like the Chicago and Northwestern Station (No. 34), it has rarely handled more than half those numbers.

Like Northwestern Station, Union Station is a model of efficient planning for a tremendous volume of traffic. Because Union Station serves two independent sets of tracks operated by different railroads, it presented an even more challenging design problem than Northwestern Station. The efficient solution was to operate passenger and cargo areas, so that all areas used by the passenger—ticket offices, baggage checks, waiting rooms, concourse, and platforms—are on one level, isolated from the level where baggage, mail, and freight are handled. Few railroad stations in the country surpass Union Station in efficiency of plan or grandeur of design.

44 35 East Wacker Drive. 1926. (Originally Jewelers Building.)

Architects: Thielbar and Fugard in association with Giaver and Dinkelberg.

This lavishly ornamented office structure was built for jewelry concerns, hence its original name (the letters "JB" are worked into the ornament extensively). The cream-colored terra-cotta that covers the building has been molded into neobaroque ornament. Atop each corner of the twenty-four-story main block is a round, domed pavilion on columns. The seventeen-story tower is crowned with a larger enclosed pavilion. Originally a parking garage occupied the central portion of each of the first twenty-two floors. A tenant could drive into the building from the lower level of Wacker Drive, enter an elevator and ride to the appropriate floor, and then park on that floor. This unique arrangement was abandoned after fourteen years for various reasons. The space occupied by the elevator shafts was then converted to office use.

45 333 North Michigan Avenue. 1928.

Architects: Holabird and Root.

Based on Eliel Saarinen's influential—but only second-prize-winning—entry in the 1922 competition for the design of Tribune Tower, this was the first of the distinctive skyscrapers built in Chicago during the late 1920s and early 1930s. These buildings are marked by their forceful verticality—achieved through successive setbacks, strongly articulated vertical piers, and long, vertical bands of windows. Building planes are flat, and smoothly finished materials are used extensively. Ornament is in very low relief and consists of highly stylized, severely geometric forms. Cornices are never used. This style of design, called Art Deco or Vertical style, freed the skyscraper from the historical forms that had shrouded it since the Columbian Exposition of 1893. The major practitioners of this style in Chicago were Graham, Anderson, Probst and White, and Holabird and Root.

This long, narrow, slablike building rises twenty-

four stories, and has a tower that rises to thirty-five stories at the northern end. Above a four-story, polished marble base, the structure is clad in limestone. Framing the windows of the fifth floor is incised ornament portraying scenes from early Chicago history. Vertical bands of windows appear on the three sides of the northern tower.

The building is superbly sited. The four structures built during the 1920s at Michigan Avenue and the Chicago River—London Guarantee, Wrigley, Tribune Tower, and 333—present a vivid capsule history of American architecture of that decade, from the Beaux-Arts classicism of the early 1920s, through the Gothic skyscrapers of mid-decade, to the Vertical style that prevailed into the early 1930s. By orienting the facade of 333 North Michigan toward the north, the architects provided a handsome termination to the vista down Michigan Avenue from Oak Street.

46 Carbide and Carbon Building. 1929.
230 North Michigan Avenue.

Architects: Burnham Brothers.

The color contrasts of the Carbide and Carbon Building make it unique among Chicago's Art Deco skyscrapers. Although many of New York's Art Deco buildings employ polychromatic materials, those in Chicago tend to be gray granite with dark metal spandrel panels. The base of the Carbide and Carbon Building is sheathed in black polished granite with black marble and bronze trim at the entrance, the tower is clad in dark green terra-cotta (now blackened by grime), and the pinnacle is trimmed in gold leaf. The finial-like forms at the top of the building are also characteristic of the Art Deco skyscrapers of New York.

47 Kemper Insurance Building. 1929. (Originally Civic Opera Building.)

20 North Wacker Drive.

Architects: Graham, Anderson, Probst and White.

Not since Adler and Sullivan's Auditorium of 1889 (No. 9) had such a project been undertaken on so large a scale: a hall for the performance of grand opera has here been incorporated into a major structure that serves other functions. The Civic Opera House was successor to the Auditorium in another way. After the Opera House opened in 1929, opera and other musical events were regularly booked here rather than at the Auditorium, which led to the eventual closing of the earlier hall.

This building is impressive for its structural achievement as well as for its architectural design. Carrying the weight of a massive office tower above a base that contains the void of two large theaters required a complex system of enormous trusses that transfer loads at various levels. In design, the building is typical of the office buildings of the late 1920s. Above the thirteenth floor of the river facade is a deep setback. The vertical bands of windows and continuous piers are also characteristic of the late 1920s. The Wacker Drive facade is a broad plane unbroken by setbacks. At its base an impressive colonnade covers the sidewalk and terminates at each end in a pedimented entrance to one of the auditoriums.

KEMPER
INSURANCE

48 Riverside Plaza. 1929.
400 West Madison Street.

Architects: Holabird and Root.

Originally the Chicago Daily News Building, this was the first Chicago building to be erected on railroad air rights, in this case on the north track layout of the recently completed Union Station. By placing the narrow office block on the west edge of the site, the architects opened half of the lot area to a broad plaza that faces the Civic Opera on the east side of the river. The simple slablike form of the steel-framed building; the vertical bands suggesting piers or pilasters at the base, end bays, and top; the blocklike masses of the wings; and the emphatic symmetry are all distinguishing features of the purified skyscraper style that flourished briefly in the late 1920s.

49 Chicago Board of Trade Building. CL, NR
1930.

141 West Jackson Boulevard.

Architects: Holabird and Root.

The Board of Trade is one of Chicago's best Art Deco skyscrapers, in large part because its massing so perfectly reinforces the perspective view down LaSalle Street and provides such a forceful termination to the LaSalle Street canyon. An earlier Board of Trade Building designed by W. W. Boyington, which occupied the same site from 1885 until 1928, also towered over its neighbors and dramatically terminated LaSalle Street.

The present structure rests on a nine-story base which contained the enormous six-story trading room of the Board (until it was divided horizontally in 1975 to provide additional space needed by the

Chicago Board Options Exchange); this space is expressed on the exterior by the tall windows above the third floor. Above the base a wide tower rises at the rear of the structure to reach forty-five stories. Two symmetrical projections to the north rise thirteen stories above the base and create a deep setback. This vertical massing is reinforced by the tall continuous piers of the towers. Horizontal lines are minimized; the spandrels of the towers are recessed and discontinuous. Atop the pyramidal roof is a 32-foot aluminum statue of Ceres, the Roman goddess of grain. Designed by sculptor John H. Stoors, it symbolizes one of the chief commodities traded by the Board.

Low entrance corridors flanked by shops lead to a high three-story lobby which is a masterpiece of Art Deco design. The space is finished in several varieties of contrasting marble, demonstrating the Art Deco fondness for sleek, polished surfaces. Translucent glass and nickel reflectors cast a diffused light that is mirrored in the marble. Throughout the lobby are examples of the severely rectilinear ornament characteristic of the Art Deco style.

50 Chicago Club Building. 1930.

81 East Van Buren Street.

Architects: Granger and Bollenbacher.

The Chicago Club formerly occupied a building on this same site which had been designed by Burnham and Root and built in 1887 as the home of the Art Institute of Chicago. After the Art Institute relocated to its present building in 1894, the Chicago Club occupied Burnham and Root's Romanesque structure until 1929. The present fortress-like, rugged Romanesque building is an appropriate bastion for one of Chicago's exclusive private clubs. It also blends well with its neighbors to the south, the Fine Arts Building (see No. 6) and the Auditorium (see No. 9).

51 **Merchandise Mart. 1930.**
The River (north bank) between Wells and Orleans streets.

Architects: Graham, Anderson, Probst and White.

Until the Pentagon was built in Washington, D.C., this was the largest building in the world in floor area. It is also notable as one of the sites of the "markets" of furniture and furnishings, attended by buyers from all over the country, in which new offerings are displayed in showrooms maintained by manufacturers. The style is "modern" of the 1920s, although the design is less impressive than many of that period.

52 LaSalle National Bank Building. 1934. (Originally Field Building)

135 South LaSalle Street.

Architects: Graham, Anderson, Probst and White.

This was the last Art Deco skyscraper built in Chicago; indeed, it was the last large office building completed before the twenty-year hiatus in major construction occasioned by the Depression and Second World War. The forms associated with the

architecture of the late 1920s have here reached a level of utter purity. Closely ranked vertical bands of windows alternate with narrow, continuous piers to create a verticality that is unrelenting. The long facade of the building extends from LaSalle to Clark, and the shorter facades appear as narrow towers facing the two streets. The central mass is forty-two stories high, and is flanked at each corner by a tower half that high. Just as the Art Deco facade pattern has here been purified, so too has the massing characteristic of that style.

A long, two-story lobby connects the LaSalle and Clark Street entrances. Finished in white, beige, and green marble complemented by metal fixtures and mirrored surfaces, it is one of Chicago's best Art Deco lobbies. At the central bank of elevators is a mail drop and elevator panel in the shape of the building itself.

The site of this building was occupied from 1884 until 1929 by the Home Insurance Building. Designed by William LeBaron Jenney, this was the first tall building supported almost entirely by a skeleton frame, and it is consequently considered the first skyscraper.

53 **Chicago Sun-Times Building. 1957.**
North Wabash Avenue at the Chicago River (north bank).

Architects: Naess and Murphy.

Built to house the *Chicago Sun-Times* and the now-defunct *Chicago Daily News,* this is an early example of a riverfront building sited to provide a pedestrian plaza overlooking the river. An earlier building occupied by the *Daily News* (now Riverside Plaza, No. 48) was the first riverfront building in Chicago to provide such a plaza. This modern newspaper plant is easily accessible to the public, and one can see the presses in operation from the hallways.

54 Inland Steel Building. 1957.
30 West Monroe Street.

Architects: Skidmore, Owings and Merrill.

The supporting columns have been placed outside the curtain wall, giving a forceful vertical emphasis. The large spans possible in modern steel construction allowed the architects to dispense with interior columns, so that complete freedom for the division or arrangement of the space of each floor was achieved. All elevators, stairs, and service facilities are located in a separate structure to the east, contributing to the freedom of the interior in the building proper and lending interest to the exterior as a whole.

55 Hartford Plaza Buildings. 1961, 1971.
100 and 150 South Wacker Drive.

Architects: Skidmore, Owings and Merrill.

These buildings demonstrate an interesting solution in one of today's chief areas for experiment: the treatment of the "wall" of a skyscraper. Here the glass is hung back deeply within a reinforced concrete frame, providing functional advantages, such as shading the glass area and giving easier access for washing it. The primary value, however, would seem to be aesthetic—the introduction of an interesting depth into the facades, a welcome contrast to the many contemporary skinlike walls. The horizontal members of the concrete frame are slightly curved on their undersides, thus greatly enlivening the design. The concrete frame is surfaced in light gray granite.

The southern building, designed by the same architects for the same owners, offers a striking contrast in color and finish of material and in treatment of the wall surface. The walls are of polished black granite and the windows have been set flush with the wall plane, creating a sleek, smooth surface. The only depth is created by the very slight outward flare of the piers at the base.

56 CNA Center. 1962, 1972.
55 East Jackson Boulevard.
325 South Wabash Avenue.

Architects: C. F. Murphy Associates (1962); Graham, Anderson, Probst and White (1972).

The earlier of these two buildings is the better design. Its extraordinarily wide bays (an unprecedented 42 feet) and forcefully articulated curtain walls place it in the finest tradition of Chicago design. The facade of the later building is much less assertive and distinguished.

57 United States Gypsum Building. 1963.
101 South Wacker Drive.

Architects: The Perkins and Will Partnership.

The nineteen-story, steel-framed tower exhibits the novel feature of being turned at 45 degrees to the street lines—a simple planning device which serves to admit light equally to all four elevations, to provide four little triangular plazas on the site, and to interrupt the solid row of fronts extending to the north and south along the drive. The building is the most richly clad of all Chicago office towers. The continuous columns, lying outside the main wall planes, are sheathed in marble; the spandrels are rough-faced slabs of black slate, and the windows are composed of dark glass with a bluish-gray tint. The ceilings above the open areas around the lobby and around the utility core at the top floor are broken up into planes forming shallow dihedral angles, and the column sheathing ends in sharp-pointed finials standing clear above the roof line. The shapes of these various polyhedra were derived from the crystalline structure of calcium sulfate, the chemical name for gypsum. The contrasts of shape, color, and texture in the building's external covering are disciplined by the geometry of the underlying frame, which thus saves it from ostentatious extravagance.

58 Federal Center. 1964, 1975.
Dearborn Street between Jackson Boulevard and Adams Street.

Architects: Mies van der Rohe; Schmidt, Garden and Erikson; C. F. Murphy Associates; A. Epstein and Sons.

One of the finest works of Ludwig Mies van der Rohe, this complex is interesting, not only for the individual buildings, but for their relationship to each other in a masterful composition around a central plaza. On the east side of Dearborn Street is the thirty-story Dirksen courthouse and office building, the first of the group to be built. The block to the west is occupied at its southern end by the forty-five-story Kluczynski office building and at the northwestern corner by a single-story post office whose lofty ceiling relates to the lobbies of the two towers. Almost one-half of the total site is plaza. The major plaza space opens to the north, where its edge is defined by Holabird and Roche's 1894 Marquette Building (No. 19), whose facade prefigures Mies's spare geometry. At the inner corner of the plaza is Alexander Calder's red-painted, spontaneous free-form stabile "Flamingo," which stands in perfect contrast to the disciplined sophistication of the dark steel and glass curtain walls.

The Federal Center is the most recent addition to the collection of architectural masterworks that line Dearborn Street from Polk to the river, and is the southernmost of the three major plazas along the street that contain large-scale works of contemporary art. Few streets in the country can match this one in terms of architecture and public art.

59 **Marina City. 1964, 1967.**
The River (north bank) between State and Dearborn streets.

Architects: Bertrand Goldberg Associates.

This tightly unified complex embraces apartments, garages, restaurants, office building, bank, marina, television studio, and theater. The two sixty-story apartment towers are of concrete construction in which the loads are carried mainly by cylindrical cores. The parking space is a helical slab rising continuously through the first eighteen stories of each tower. The pie-shaped rooms extend into rings of semicircular balconies, which transform the smooth cylinders into lively repetitive patterns.

60 Brunswick Building. 1965.
69 West Washington Street.

Architects: Skidmore, Owings and Merrill.

Unlike most of its contemporary neighbors, the thirty-eight-story Brunswick Building employs load-bearing exterior walls. Because the building loads are supported by these concrete screen walls and by a shear-wall core, the interior spaces are column-free. At the base, loads are transferred from the screen wall to ten perimeter columns by means of an enormous (1½-story) transfer girder. This creates an openness at the ground floor that would not have existed had the screen wall been carried to grade level. A slight inward curve above the base provides a transition between the massive girder and the open screen wall above it. Unfortunately, the ground-floor piers are sheathed in travertine and the girder in high-density paneled concrete, materials that do not harmonize with the screen wall and consequently detract from the design.

61 **Richard J. Daley Center. 1965. (Originally Civic Center.)**
Block bounded by Washington, Randolph, Dearborn, and Clark streets.

Architects: C. F. Murphy Associates; Loebl, Schlossman and Bennett; Skidmore, Owings and Merrill.

The structural bays of this thirty-one-story building are tremendously large: an unprecedented 87 feet long and almost 48 feet wide. The perimeter columns, spandrels, and mullions are of self-weathering Cor-ten steel that over the years has turned a deep russet color; windows are amber glass. Note that the cruciform columns become narrower as they rise higher, reflecting the greater weight of the frame at the base and the minimum weight at the top. The architects have exploited the Miesian idiom with verve and finesse.

The building houses courtrooms and offices, and is sited at the northern part of the block to allow for a large plaza intended for civic functions and public use. A sculpture executed in Cor-ten steel from a design given to the city by Pablo Picasso dominates the plaza. The building and its plaza were renamed after the death of the late Mayor Richard J. Daley.

62 Equitable Building. 1965.
North Michigan at the River.

Architects: Skidmore, Owings and Merrill; Alfred Shaw, Associated.

Noteworthy for the collaboration of owners and architects in reserving a large area as a plaza, in a downtown commercial building, thus achieving an openness all too often lacking in skyscrapers that are built to the legal limit of the lot area.

The design is interesting in the way it explores the possibilities of the four-window scheme—the outer two windows narrower than the inner ones—which was used with such subtlety in the 860–880 Lake Shore Drive Apartments. Here the difference in width is more obvious, and the effect thus perhaps more dramatic. A pleasant tension arises in each group of four windows from the contrast of the central pair, which are nearly square, with the outer pair, which are clearly vertical rectangles. The horizontal strip of greenish-black marble below the windows adds very different horizontal rectangles which echo the horizontals of the floors. This interesting tension, or play of shapes, helps give the building a "presence" often lacking in contemporary buildings and aided here by the warm tonality coming from the beige color of the aluminum sheathing and the light bronze-tinted glass. The projecting verticals of the exterior not only set the larger units of the design but are also used in practical ways. For instance, the "piers" between the groups of four windows, although not structural—being merely shells set outside the structural piers—carry inside them cylindrical conduits through which hot or cold air is pumped to the offices from floors housing machinery at the top and bottom of the building.

63 Connecticut Mutual Life Building. 1966.
33 North Dearborn Street.

Architects: Skidmore, Owings and Merrill.

This facade expresses the steel frame in a straightforward manner that places it firmly in the tradition of the Chicago School. The tripartite window division recalls that of the Chicago window. Floor heights and bay widths relate well to those of the building to the south. The frame is sheathed in polished black granite, except at the base where the piers are clad in travertine. This gives the building an incongruous top-heavy appearance. The ground floor is bisected by a pedestrian walkway that leads to a small pocket plaza at the east, containing Tony Smith's sculptural composition "Wandering Rocks."

CANDIES

64 Ryan Insurance Building. 1968.

(Originally Blue Cross–Blue Shield Building.)

55 West Wacker Drive.

Architects: C. F. Murphy Associates.

Structure is forcefully expressed in this ruggedly handsome fifteen-story concrete building. The eight wide columns around the perimeter, each paired with a narrower column, act in conjunction with the massive core to support the building. The wider columns also encase heating and air conditioning ducts. All vertical elements were bush hammered to give them a rough-textured surface; closely ranked, narrow striations emphasize their verticality. In contrast, all horizontal elements are smooth surfaced. A nice balance has been achieved between the strong vertical columns and the horizontal spandrels and heavy cornice. The concrete was specially tinted to achieve a warm beige color.

This building was planned as an administrative center for the Blue Cross–Blue Shield health insurance programs, which quickly outgrew it. Because the lobby was used for policy inquiries and service, it is more spacious than many office building lobbies. The central core, which carries elevators and stairs, is of bush-hammered concrete, and the waffled ceiling of the lobby is smooth-surfaced concrete. The exterior aesthetic—smooth-surfaced horizontals and rough-surfaced verticals—is thereby carried through to the interior.

RYAN
INSURANCE

65 Seventeenth Church of Christ, Scientist. 1968.

Heald Square, East Wacker Drive at Wabash Avenue.

Architects: Harry Weese and Associates.

A powerful semicircular form enables this low church building to hold its own on a visually prominent site surrounded by taller structures. This assertive form also expresses the major interior space: a large, rounded auditorium where religious services are conducted. The auditorium rests on reinforced concrete columns and girders clearly visible at ground level. A bronze-and-glass lobby is recessed behind a sunken plaza. The plaza serves not only to isolate the lobby from traffic and passersby, but also to admit natural light to the Sunday School rooms below grade level. Most of the structure is reinforced concrete sheathed in travertine. Steel girders encased in travertine support the lead-coated cooper roof and are a major element of the design. Long, slotlike windows at the base of the conical roof admit natural light to the auditorium, as do the windows at the base of the drum that crowns the roof. To the east is a seven-story triangular wing that contains church offices and meeting rooms, restrooms and lounges, and elevators and mechanical areas.

66 **First National Bank Building. 1969.**
Madison Street between Dearborn and Clark streets.

Architects: C. F. Murphy Associates; The Perkins and Will Partnership.

The most conspicuous feature of this 850-foot-high building is the inward-sweeping curve of the columns that stand outside the long elevations. The choice of the shape arises from sound functional planning. The maximum floor area is required at the street and mezzanine levels, where commercial banking facilities serve the heaviest public traffic. Above the base other banking activi-

ties dictated a smaller but still extensive floor area. The space above, which is rented to tenants, meets their needs for perimeter offices and less floor area. At the very top of the building a longitudinal row of separate penthouses encloses various mechanical and electrical utilities. Elevator shafts, stairs, main ducts, and pipes are housed in utility cores placed at both ends of the building to allow maximum open banking space.

This hierarchical arrangement of functions, as one of the designing architects called it, compelled a marked deviation from the standard prismatic form of the skyscraper. A tapering envelope would provide maximum resistance to the horizontal forces of wind, but an upward-curving one would preserve the structural and functional validity while achieving the most graceful form. The steel framing members of the bank building are sheathed in gray-speckled granite, harmonizing nicely with the bronze-tinted glass. The powerfully articulated walls stand squarely in the Chicago tradition.

67 IBM Building. 1971.

The River (north bank) between Wabash and State Streets.

Architects: Office of Mies van der Rohe and C. F. Murphy Associates.

This is the last office building designed by Ludwig Mies van der Rohe, and a bust of the architect is in the high-ceilinged, travertine and glass lobby.

The superbly proportioned tower with its precisely detailed curtain wall achieves the elegant simplicity characteristic of the architect's work during the last decades of his life. This refined simplicity belies the complex problems of this particular site. For its regional office building in Chicago, IBM acquired a K-shaped riverfront site bisected at grade level by a railroad spur. Initially, a U-shaped structure was planned, but the city agreed to eliminate part of Wabash Avenue so that the site would better accommodate a rectangular structure. On-site parking requirements were modified because the rail tracks beneath the structure made it impossible to provide the required spaces. However, a parking garage sheathed in Cor-ten steel was designed by George Schipporeit and built just to the north in 1972.

The tower is fifty-two stories high and has a curtain wall of dark aluminum and bronze-tinted glass. The bays of the structural steel skeleton are 30 feet wide and 40 feet long. The mechanical systems of the building are extremely sophisticated, in large part because of the controlled environment necessary for areas housing computers. Temperatures are controlled by a computer, and the heat given off by lights, machines, and people inside the building is reclaimed by a reverse refrigeration cycle. Heat transfer between exterior and interior is reduced by a plastic thermal barrier that separates the curtain wall from the frame.

The building occupies a prominent riverfront site. Unfortunately, however, the plaza takes little advantage of the site. No link to the riverfront is provided, and only a dull granite wall meets the river.

68 Sears Tower. 1974.
Block bounded by Franklin Street and Wacker Drive, Adams Street, and Jackson Boulevard.

Architects: Skidmore, Owings and Merrill.

The bold stepped-back silhouette of the Sears Tower dominates Chicago's skyline with strength and élan. At 1,468 feet (110 stories), it is the

world's tallest building, exceeding New York's twin-towered World Trade Center by 100 feet and Chicago's Standard Oil Building by 330 feet. The structural steel frame is sheathed in black aluminum and bronze-tinted glass. The structure consists of nine framed tubes, each 75 feet square. These tubes are banded together structurally to form a mega-tube that provides lateral strength to withstand wind loads. The nine tubes rise together for forty-nine stories, where the northwest and southeast tubes terminate. The building rises as a Z through the next sixteen stories. At the sixty-fifth floor, the northeast and southwest tubes stop, and the building continues as a cruciform to the ninetieth floor. There, the remaining north, east, and south tubes end, creating a rectangular tower that rises twenty stories to reach the full height. This aesthetically dynamic series of setbacks is functionally practical. The corporate headquarters of Sears, Roebuck and Company occupies the base of the building, where it requires maximum floor area. The upper floors are meant to accommodate future expansion. In the interim they are rented to tenants, and consequently a larger perimeter area with outside exposure is necessary. The resulting pattern of setbacks and the flush wall planes recall the skyscrapers of the late 1920s and early 1930s.

The building rests on an uninspired granite plaza. Its dullness is offset, however, by the colorful whimsy of Alexander Calder's spiraling and swinging sculptural creation "Universe," located in the lobby.

69 **Standard Oil Building and Plaza. 1974.**
200 East Randolph Street.

Architects: Edward Durell Stone and The Perkins and Will Partnership.

This slender steel structure faced with light gray marble is the corporate headquarters of the Standard Oil Company of Indiana. The eighty-story building lacks human scale, a serious fault in a structure this tall.

The triangular sections of marble contain the bulk of mechanical services such as the utilities and air conditioning, thus permitting flush window walls inside the building.

The tower faces Grant Park, where it rises above street level to a height of 1,136 feet. It is set back 140 feet from Randolph Street and its horizontal dimensions are 194 by 194 feet. All in all, the building contains a gross area of 2.7 million square feet.

A truly delightful lower-level plaza encircled by a restaurant and lobby contains a fascinating reflecting pool and "Sounding" sculpture by Harry Bertoia. It consists of eleven separate units, each composed of tall clusters of hard copper alloy rods welded to a naval brass plate and mounted on 18-inch pedestals of black granite. A light breeze starts the rods' movements, which in turn produce swishing sounds.

70 Metropolitan Detention Center. 1975.
Van Buren Street between Clark and Federal streets.

Architects: Harry Weese and Associates.

Located just a block away from the U.S. District Courthouse, the Metropolitan Detention Center was built to accommodate persons awaiting trial and testifying at trials as well as other short-term detainees. A humanitarian approach to the design was called for. The triangular shape of the build-

ing allows maximum perimeter space so that each inmate's room can have a 5-inch-wide window (the maximum allowed without bars by the Bureau of Prisons); window openings are splayed outward to allow a better view. The triangular shape also minimizes interior corridor space that requires surveillance. Stairwells and elevator cores are located in the corners.

The lower eleven floors contain administrative and medical facilities and mechanical equipment. The upper floors are divided into two-story self-contained units with inmates' rooms arranged around common lounge, dining, and visitors' areas. The roof houses a walled, landscaped exercise yard. Exposed reinforced concrete and articulated construction joints underscore the essentially utilitarian design of this dramatic structure. The site also accommodates a seven-story garage to the south and a triangular landscaped plaza to the northeast.

Near North Area

71 **Episcopal Cathedral of St. James. 1857.**
Wabash Avenue and Huron Street.

Architects: Burling and Bacchus (1857); Burling and Adler (1897); Chapel of St. Andrew: Ralph Adams Cram and Bertram G. Goodhue (1913); Parish House: James Hammond and Peter Roesch (1968).

The parish of St. James was organized in 1834, making it the oldest Episcopal parish in Chicago and one of the oldest in Illinois. This church became the cathedral of the Episcopal Diocese of Chicago in 1955. Parts of the present structure date from 1857, when the church first located at this corner. The Chicago Fire of 1871 destroyed most of the church, and it was rebuilt in 1874–75. It was designed in an English Gothic style and built of Joliet limestone. The small chapel of St. Andrew is based on a small abbey chapel in southern Scotland and reportedly contains glass and stone from that Scottish chapel. To the east is the contemporary Parish House, which has a clearly articulated and carefully detailed curtain wall in the best contemporary tradition. It is set back from Huron Street, opening a small plaza to the east of the cathedral.

72 Old Chicago Water Tower. 1869. CL, NR
North Michigan Avenue at Chicago Avenue.

Architect: W. W. Boyington.

Built to house a 138-foot standpipe that was required to equalize the pressure of the water being pumped from the Pumping Station to the east, the Old Chicago Water Tower was designed by one of Chicago's earliest architects. Boyington's imitation of Gothic architecture is so naive that it seems original at points, as in the cut-stone "battlements" at the top of the lower wall sections. Oscar Wilde, on his visit to Chicago in 1882, called it a "castellated monstrosity with pepper boxes stuck all over it," although he praised the pumping machinery as "simple, grand and natural." It is one of the few buildings that survived in the path of the Chicago Fire of 1871. The Old Water Tower occupies a commanding position on Chicago's most prominent avenue and serves as a tourist information center.

73 Holy Name Cathedral. 1874.
NE corner of State and Superior streets.

Architect: Patrick Charles Keely; remodeled by Henry J. Schlacks (1915); renovation by C. F. Murphy and Associates (1969).

Holy Name has served as the cathedral of the Roman Catholic Archdiocese of Chicago since 1874. The parish itself began in 1846, at which time it worshiped in the Chapel of the Holy Name on the first floor of the University of St. Mary of the Lake, which then occupied this site. The present church replaced an earlier Gothic edifice that had been built in 1854 and was destroyed by the Chicago Fire of 1871. The structure is limestone and its design is simple Late Victorian Gothic. A major renovation was undertaken in 1969; at the time the original foundation was replaced by one of reinforced concrete.

74 Old Town Triangle District. **CL**

Bounded roughly by North Avenue, Lincoln Park, and the extension of Ogden Avenue north to Armitage Avenue.

This distinctive area was settled in the 1850s primarily by working-class German families who built modest frame houses of the type now known as "Chicago cottages." The Chicago cottage could be built quickly and easily because it employs a balloon frame, an innovative structural system developed in Chicago in the 1830s. Instead of the heavy timber posts and beams secured by mortise-and-tenon joints that formed the traditional wooden frame, the balloon frame used ready-cut lumber and machine-made nails. The Chicago cottage is either 1½ or 2½ stories high and has a pitched roof with gable ends at front and rear. It usually has a high basement and a raised front entrance placed next to a pair of windows. Usually quite

plain but occasionally somewhat ornate, these structures continued to be built in the area until an 1874 fire ordinance prohibited construction of frame buildings within the city limits. Later many row houses were built in the area, usually either Italianate or Queen Anne in style. A row of five houses at 1826–34 North Lincoln Park West was designed by Louis Sullivan and built in 1885. These houses display the pseudo-Egyptian ornament Sullivan had learned while in the employ of Philadelphia architect Frank Furness. Old Town experienced a period of decline earlier in this century, but in the late 1940s one of the earliest neighborhood revitalization efforts in this country began there. During the past thirty years, many houses in Old Town have been rehabilitated, and the scale and charm of the neighborhood have been preserved.

75 Mid-North District. **CL**

Bounded generally by Fullerton Avenue, Clark Street, Armitage Avenue, and Lincoln Avenue and Orchard Street.

Fullerton Avenue was the northern boundary of Chicago when Mid-North began to develop as a residential area around the middle of the nineteenth century. The fire that destroyed the city in 1871 died out in this vicinity because here the frame houses were more widely separated than those closer to the river. Three of the four houses in Mid-North that survived the fire still stand: the Policeman Bellinger cottage at 2121 North Hudson Street, and the two houses at 2339 and 2343 North Cleveland. After the fire, brick row houses and free-standing residences were built, giving Mid-North the late-nineteenth-century urban character

that still prevails. Within the district, the double-bayed house at 440 West Belden was designed by Louis Sullivan in 1883, and another house at 2147 Cleveland has been attributed to him. Mid-North also has a large number of contemporary structures that are sympathetic in scale and materials to the older buildings.

76 Astor Street District. **CL**

North Astor Street between East Division Street and East North Boulevard.

Astor Street developed as the heart of Chicago's fashionable Gold Coast area beginning in the 1880s. The earliest house on the six-block street (named for John Jacob Astor) is the large Queen Anne mansion at North Boulevard, designed by Alfred F. Pashley in 1880 as the residence of the Catholic Archbishop of Chicago. Still occupied by Chicago's archbishop, the house displays a lively profusion of bays, dormers, gables, and the chimneys typical of the Queen Anne style. In 1882, Potter Palmer built his imposing residence, designed by Cobb and Frost, on Lake Shore Drive between Banks and Schiller streets (demolished in 1950), and soon the area became as fashionable as Prairie Avenue had formerly been. During the next several decades, wealthy Chicagoans commissioned many prominent architects to design townhouses along Astor and adjacent streets.

The largest house on Astor Street stands at the northwest corner of Burton and Astor. In 1892, *Chicago Tribune* publisher Joseph Medill commissioned New York architect Stanford White to design this finely proportioned Renaissance revival house as a wedding gift for his daughter and son-in-law, the Robert W. Pattersons. Cyrus Hall McCormick II, a later owner of the house, commissioned David Adler to design an addition to the north, more than doubling the size of the house. Adler's addition so precisely follows White's design that the addition is barely discernible from the original structure.

Unlike the Patterson House, most other Astor

Street residences are compact, albeit substantial, townhouses. Among the most notable are the James Charnley House at 1365 North Astor (No. 79), designed by Frank Lloyd Wright while he was employed by Adler and Sullivan; the neo-Elizabethan James Houghteling houses at 1308–12 Astor, designed by John Wellborn Root in 1887; the French Renaissance revival Joseph T. Ryerson House at 1406, designed by David Adler in 1922; and the contemporary house at 1524, designed in 1968 by I. W. Colburn, which so completely respects its neighbors and the scale of the street.

Three Art Deco structures on the street date from the late 1920s and early 1930s: the Edward P. Russell House at 1444 Astor, designed by Holabird and Root in 1929, and two apartment buildings at 1301 and 1260, designed by Philip B. Maher in 1929 and 1930, respectively.

Apartment buildings had first appeared on Astor Street with Holabird and Roche's 1897 McConnell Apartments at 1210 Astor. This straightforward Chicago School structure is not unlike the commercial office buildings this firm was designing for downtown Chicago at the time, and it incorporates several similar features. It was not until the 1950s, however, that a proliferation of high-rise apartment buildings began to intrude upon the scale of the area. Few of these compare in elegance to Bertrand Goldberg's 1962 Astor Tower at 1300 Astor, and most seem like clumsy giants next to their urbane late nineteenth- and early twentieth-century neighbors.

77 McCormick Row House District. 1882–89. CL
Between Belden and Fullerton avenues, Halsted Street, and the elevated tracks.

Architect: A. M. F. Colton and Son.

These brick row houses were built as rental units to supplement the endowment of McCormick Theological Seminary. Founded in Indiana in 1829 as the Indiana Theological Seminary, this Presbyterian institution moved to Chicago thirty years later with the promise of financial assistance from Cyrus Hall McCormick, inventor of the reaper. Construction of the campus began in 1862, although the row houses were not built until twenty years later. The houses fronting on Belden and Fullerton avenues were the first constructed. They are a simplified Queen Anne style with a varied roof line, ornamental brickwork, and contrasting stone trim. The houses facing away from these and fronting on Chalmers Place, a quiet street bordering a small private park, were built in the late 1880s. These later houses are quite severe: cleanly incised window openings and deeply recessed door openings are set simply into the broad facade which is of brown brick trimmed in brown stone. A symmetrical arrangement of round and triangular gables marks the roof line. In 1973, McCormick Seminary left its North Side campus to affiliate with the theology schools at the University of Chicago. The row houses were then sold to private owners.

78 Nickerson Residence. 1883. CL, NR
40 East Erie Street.

Architects: Burling and Whitehouse.

One of the lavish houses of the eighties and well preserved, this classical structure was perhaps inspired by Parisian townhouses. The interiors offer fascinating examples of the use of period styles in such houses at the time. The owner was one of the early art collectors of Chicago, and the Art Institute of Chicago now has in its collections works that doubtless appeared at one time in the "gallery" that formed a part of this house.

79 James Charnley House. 1892. CL, NR
1365 North Astor Street.

Architects: Adler and Sullivan; Frank Lloyd Wright.

Officially by the firm of Adler and Sullivan, this house is believed to have been designed by Wright while in their employ. The closed-up, blocky design is in marked contrast to Wright's later "Prairie" houses (see No. 144). The shallow brick and cut stone are the background for the very formal design, of which the obvious elements are the door and the small windows. The balcony, in its lightness and openness, contrasts with the solid mass of the house. Despite its shallowness, it perhaps puts an excessive emphasis on the center of a short facade (contrast No. 80). A later extension of the facade to the right, in the porches built there, obscures its original symmetry.

80 Fortnightly of Chicago. 1892. CL, NR
(Originally the Bryan Lathrop House.)
120 East Bellevue Street.

Architects: McKim, Mead and White.

The unusually fine facade in the classic manner shows that this building is related to the Georgian style of the eighteenth century. The shallow relieving arches over the openings of the first floor, the scale of the decoration over the three central ones, the relative emphasis in the two string courses and the cornice, and the vigor given by the projection of the ample bays at each end are the most obvious features of a masterly design, clear, open, urbane. In part because of the placing of the door, the facade carries its symmetry easily, without rigidity or undue emphasis. The length of the central window of the third floor, which breaks the string course below the other windows here, was related to a light, openwork balcony outside it, now removed; similar balconies were outside the three central windows of the second floor.

81 Newberry Library. 1892.
60 West Walton Street.

Architect: Henry Ives Cobb.

Housing one of the great research collections of the Midwest, the library was built to the specifications of a strong-minded librarian who insisted on such features as hallways constructed almost as separate buildings, in order to preserve quiet in the reading rooms. The massive, Romanesque style follows H. H. Richardson's example and was used by Cobb in several other buildings of Chicago and vicinity, such as the former home of the Chicago Historical Society (No. 82).

82 Second Chicago Historical Society Building. Begun 1892.

632 North Dearborn Street.

Architect: Henry Ives Cobb.

This building was the second permanent home of the Chicago Historical Society. Organized in 1856, when the city itself was only nineteen years old, the historical society purchased this site in 1865. Its first permanent building, designed by Burling and Whitehouse (see also No. 78), was completed in 1868 and destroyed in the Chicago Fire three years later. Work on the present structure began in 1892. This rugged building is a handsome example of the Romanesque revival style made popular by Henry Hobson Richardson (see No. 118). Its rough-hewn granite facade, rounded turrets with conical roofs, and bands of arched and transomed windows are typical of the style. The historical society was located here until 1931, when it moved to its present location in Lincoln Park.

83 Brewster Apartments. 1893.
2800 North Pine Grove.

Architect: Enoch Hill Turnock.

The narrow windows and the rough-faced granite blocks of the wall make the Brewster in its external appearance a rather traditional and somewhat romanticized version of the oriel-windowed apartment buildings of the Chicago School. The interior design, however, represents a bold solution to the problem of admitting natural light to the spaces inside the building. In plan it is a hollow rectangle, the inner court of which is surmounted by a gabled skylight—a common form for the multistory office block in the nineteenth century, but one which posed a peculiar difficulty in the case of an apartment building. To provide access to upper-floor apartments from a single centrally located elevator, Turnock introduced a little pedestrian bridge running the length of the court in each floor, with lateral branches extending to the individual entrance doors. The bridge decks are composed of glass blocks supported by light steel girders at the edges. The thin frames of these translucent bridges and the open grillwork of the elevator shaft form a vivid pattern of black lines set off against the diffused light falling from the glass roof above the court.

84 Tree Studios. 1894. NR

North State Street between Ohio and Ontario streets.

Architects: Hill and Woltersdorf (1894); Woltersdorf and Bernhard (1912, 1913).

This four-story yellow Roman brick building with limestone trim around windows and doorways was a precursor of the many loft-building apartments scattered around the Loop. The high ceilings and large glass windows make these ideal artists' studios as well as comfortable living areas. The carefully worked out stone detail expresses a freedom from classical forms.

The interior garden area gives those fortunate tenants who face it a delightful green and open space in the very heart of the city. This fascinating and delightful building was constructed by Judge Lambert Tree.

85 Francis J. Dewes House. 1896. CL, NR
503 West Wrightwood Avenue.

Architects: Adolph Cudell and Arthur Hercz.

This baroque revival house and its smaller neighbor to the west were built by a wealthy German brewer who fondly recalled the architecture of his native land and who hired two European architects who shared his recollection of baroque buildings. Because the Dewes House is by no means enormous, it was important that the elaborate ornament be carefully handled and placed so that it would not overwhelm the simple cubic structure. The major ornament is therefore reserved for the largest element of the facade: the central entrance bay on Wrightwood, with its sinuous caryatids supporting the second-floor balcony; the angled bay at the northeast corner of the house; and the bay containing the large stained- and leaded-glass staircase window on the west facade. Note especially the finely carved stonework and the intricately detailed cast-iron railings. These railings were originally complemented by the elaborate fence that ran in front of the yard separating the two houses.

86 Theurer/Wrigley House. 1896. **CL**
2466 North Lakeview Avenue.

Architect: Richard E. Schmidt.

The Theurer/Wrigley House is an early work of Richard E. Schmidt and, possibly, his chief draftsman, Hugh M. Garden. Schmidt and Garden later became prominent Prairie School architects, producing such designs as the Albert Madlener House (No. 87) and the Montgomery Ward warehouse (No. 89). The Theurer/Wrigley House is a more traditional design. Its massing is reminiscent of an Italian Renaissance palazzo, and its ornament derives from baroque precedents. The house is of Roman brick with stone and terra-cotta trim. The copper cornice and roof have acquired a green patina, providing an unusual color contrast to the rest of the building. Joseph Theurer, for whom the house was built, was president of the Schoenhofen Brewery and later commissioned Schmidt to design a powerhouse for that company. It still stands and is one of Schmidt's best designs (No. 111). This house was subsequently purchased by the Wrigley family, manufacturers of chewing gum.

87 Madlener House. 1902. CL, NR
(Now the Graham Foundation for Advanced Studies in the Fine Arts.)
4 West Burton Place.

Architect: Richard E. Schmidt.

This clear, cubical mass is as forceful as a Florentine palace. There is an interesting variety in the various emphases on the horizontal, in stone base, string courses, and grouping of the windows. The decoration around the door is a fine example of modern ornament, similar to Sullivan's geometric type. The interior has been remodeled and restored for the Graham Foundation by Brenner, Danforth and Rockwell.

88 Holy Trinity Russian Orthodox Cathedral. 1903. **CL, NR**

1121 North Leavitt Street.

Architect: Louis H. Sullivan.

The Cathedral is interesting as a work in a traditional form by the "prophet of modern architecture." The basic form is that of Russian churches, derived from the earlier Byzantine architecture. The plan is a central type, basically a square with extensions at ground level, the central space crowned with a dome. In the interior the proportions of the space—small, but with relatively large arches—the painted decoration, and the shallow dome combine to produce an effect of delicacy and refinement, as of a richly decorated coffer or jewel box. The exterior is simple, with occasional exotic touches in curved shapes or angular window hoods. The exotic becomes more obvious in the onionlike shape above the lantern, which must be inspired by the bulbous domes found in Russian church architecture. Ornament is very sparingly used, the most striking appearance being in the cut-out ornament in wood over the entrance, similar to that originally in the interior of the Carson Pirie Scott Store (No. 25).

89 Montgomery Ward and Company Warehouse. 1907. NR

618 West Chicago Avenue.

Architects: Schmidt, Garden and Martin; administration building: Minoru Yamasaki and Associates (1974).

This was one of the earliest reinforced concrete buildings in the United States and was the largest reinforced concrete structure in the world at the time of its completion. The powerful horizontality of the long facade is strengthened by projecting strips at the top and bottom of each spandrel. The spandrels are faced with brick which was originally unpainted. This lent additional horizontal emphasis, but the effect was lost when the brick was painted to match the concrete. The ornament is interesting and restrained. The sober effect of strength created by the structure is a good expression of the reinforced concrete construction. The concrete frame of the later Yamasaki administration is sheathed in travertine.

90 1550 North State Parkway. 1912.

Architects: Marshall and Fox.

This elegant apartment building was designed by a firm noted for its luxury hotels and apartments. Benjamin Marshall and Charles E. Fox practiced together from 1905 until Fox's death in 1926. During that time they designed the Blackstone Hotel (1909; No. 32) and the Blackstone Theater (60 East Balbo; 1911), the apartment building at 999 North Lake Shore Drive (1912), the Edgewater Beach Hotel (1916; demolished 1969), and the Drake Hotel (1920; No. 96). The building at 1550 originally had a single fifteen-room apartment per floor. The principal living rooms—a central "petit salon" flanked on one side by the "grand salon" with a rounded bay and on the other by a dining room and "orangerie"—were arranged along the north side of the building, overlooking Lincoln Park. This provided a continuous sequence of formal spaces over 100 feet long. The bedrooms spanned the east side of the building and had a view of the lake. The kitchen, service rooms, and servants' quarters were located at the southwest section of the building. Its enormous, high-ceilinged apartments and dignified Beaux-Arts facade made this one of Chicago's finest apartment buildings during the years it housed such prominent families as the Fields and Shedds.

91 Fourth Presbyterian Church and Parish House. 1912. **NR**

125 East Chestnut Street.

Architects: Ralph Adams Cram and Howard Van Doren Shaw.

Ralph Adams Cram was one of the leaders of the Gothic revival in the United States, and his Fourth Presbyterian Church demonstrates an accurate knowledge of the Gothic style that contrasts with the naive imitation of the style found in earlier buildings such as Holy Family Church (No. 109) and the Old Chicago Water Tower (No. 72). However, the Gothic features are here modified, as in the narrowness of the side aisles, the shape of the piers, and the use of the transept space for a balcony, suggesting that the architect allowed himself some degree of freedom. The severity of the exterior contrasts with the warmer and more varied wall surfaces of the adjacent parish house by Howard Van Doren Shaw. The church is separated from the parish house by a cloistered walk and serene courtyard that seem miles away from busy North Michigan Avenue.

92 Medinah Temple. 1912.
600 North Wabash Avenue.

Architects: Hoehl and Schmid.

The Medinah Temple is the home of the Shriners of Chicago. Like many similar lodges throughout the United States, they have adopted the architecture, costumes, and rituals of the Islamic nations of the Middle East.

The temple has a central onion-shaped dome with two lesser ones on either side, each topped by a black metal crescent. Large brown striated bricks are interspersed with Moorish arches that contain small stained-glass windows of delicate floral designs.

Over the entrance can be seen a huge hemispheric beige metal grill with stone trim. Framing the grill work and stone trim is an Islamic design in colorful stone and arabic letters that, combined with the arch above and the canopy below, makes a dramatic portal for the building.

93 2700 North Lakeview Avenue. 1915.

Architects: David Adler, Henry Dangler, and Ambrose Cramer.

The southernmost two houses in this row of four were designed by David Adler, an architect who is noted for his palatial houses in the North Shore suburbs. The third house was owned and planned by Henry Dangler, with whom Adler collaborated and shared an office between 1912 and 1917. The northernmost house was owned and planned by Ambrose Cramer, an architect who worked with Adler and Dangler. All four houses have a unified facade of dark red brick above a limestone base. These stately Georgian structures recall row houses along formal squares in London and Bath.

94 Navy Pier. 1916. CL

Grand Avenue and Streeter Drive.

Architect: Charles Sumner Frost; renovation by Jerome R. Butler, Jr., City Architect (1976).

Daniel Hudson Burnham's Chicago Plan of 1909 called for two piers extending far into Lake Michigan, each providing both docking and recreational facilities. Only the north pier was ever constructed. Navy Pier is 3,000 feet long. At its west end is the twin-towered headhouse containing office space. Beyond that, for most of the length of the pier, extend two parallel two-story sheds originally used for docking and storage. The sheds are separated by a central court that contained its own streetcar line to provide public access to the recreational spaces at the east end of the pier. At the far end is a large semicircular auditorium space with a domed ceiling supported by radial trusses in the form of half arches.

The pier flourished until the 1930s when shipping traffic on the Great Lakes dwindled. During World War II, the pier was used as a Navy training facility. From 1946 until 1965, it served as the Chicago branch of the University of Illinois. After the university built its Near West Side campus, the pier went largely unused until 1976 when the City of Chicago undertook a major renovation. Since that time, city-sponsored programs at the pier have made it once again a lively and unique recreational facility.

95 Quigley Seminary. 1918.
Chestnut and Rush streets.

Architect: Gustav Steinbeck.

This neo-Gothic preparatory seminary was established in 1905 by Archbishop James E. Quigley, and construction was carried out after his death by Cardinal George Mundelein. A memorial statue of Archbishop Quigley stands at the corner of Rush and Chestnut.

Architect Steinbeck of New York carried out a design that reflected fifteenth- and early sixteenth-century French Gothic precedents. The rose window over the chapel entrance, the sculpture on either side, the high pitched roofs, the buttresses on Chestnut Street, and the medieval courtyard express an attempt by the architect and owner to reproduce a medieval setting for learning. It is reminiscent of the Palais de Justice built in Rouen between 1492 and 1508 and also of the Hotel de Cluny in Paris, built between 1485 and 1498.

96 Drake Hotel. 1920.
Lake Shore Drive, Michigan Avenue, and Walton Street.

Architects: Marshall and Fox.

This magnificent hotel occupies one of the finest locations in the city, facing Lake Michigan and the Oak Street Beach on the north, Michigan Avenue on the west, and Walton Street, where its main entrance is located, to the north. The architects, Marshall and Fox, were very generous in planning this thirteen-story limestone structure. The lobby and public rooms were designed in the grand manner, with generous spaces for dining, strolling, shopping, and resting. The guest rooms and corridors are equally generous in size, with large windows that permit excellent views, especially over Lake Michigan.

97 Elks National Memorial Building. 1926.
2750 Lakeview Avenue.

Architects: Main building, Egerton Swartwout; Magazine Building, Holabird and Root (1967).

The central, dominating unit of the structure is circular, massive in proportions, and surmounted by a flattened dome, 115 feet above the main level. Entered by a single great arched doorway, entirely encircled at a height of 38 feet by a stately colonnade which surmounts a belting frieze carved in high relief, this central building constitutes the memorial feature of the edifice.

Sculptures are by three outstanding artists of their day, Adolph A. Weinman, James Earle Fraser, and his wife, Laura Gardin Fraser. Murals are by Edwin H. Blashfield and Eugene Savage, both of whom were considered leaders in their field. The distance from the interior bronze star set in the marble floor to the dome of the rotunda is 100 feet. Marble from all over the world was used in the interior of the lavish, Roman-styled, Pantheon-like structure.

98 Playboy Building. 1930.
(Originally Palmolive Building.)

919 North Michigan Avenue.

Architects: Holabird and Root.

This is the northernmost of the Chicago skyscrapers designed in the purified Vertical style of the late 1920s and early 1930s. When the building was constructed, the area around it was developed with much lower structures, and for many years its wide facade dominated the vista up Michigan Avenue from the River. Its many symmetrical setbacks create a lively pattern of receding masses. Vertical bands of windows set into recessed channels emphasize the strong verticality. Atop the building is a 150-foot airplane beacon originally named for Charles A. Lindbergh. It no longer functions as a guide for airplanes as taller buildings have made it obsolete for navigation purposes.

99 Chicago Historical Society. 1932.
North Clark Street and North Avenue.

Architects: Graham, Anderson, Probst and White; addition by Alfred Shaw and Associates (1972).

This red brick Georgian revival structure is the fourth home occupied by the Chicago Historical Society since it was founded in 1856 (see No. 82). The columned portico and long symmetrical wings of the east facade blend gracefully with the Lincoln Park site. A mausoleum-like addition to the west is faceless and insensitive, although an attempt was apparently made to echo the columned portico of the east facade.

100 Frank Fisher Apartments. 1938.
1209 North State Parkway.

Architect: Andrew N. Rebori.

The facade of this small apartment building is similar to that of the townhouses at 1328 North State, which the same architect had designed one year earlier. Both are examples of the Art Moderne style that flourished during the 1930s. Curved windows that wrap around rounded corners and the extensive use of glass blocks, then a new material, give a "streamlined" look to buildings of this style. The ornament and textured treatment of the brick are not characteristic of the style but add visual interest.

101 860–80 Lake Shore Drive Apartments. 1952.
860–80 North Lake Shore Drive.

Architects: Mies van der Rohe; Pace Associates; Holsman, Holsman, Klekamp and Taylor.

These apartments are universally admired for their openness and the frank expression of the steel frame; and experts are further intrigued by the refinement of the design, including the subtle distribution of emphasis between the horizontal and the vertical. Especially notable are the small I-beams between the main supports, which give restrained emphasis to the vertical and also have a secondary structural value in stiffening the glass walls that surround each apartment. An interesting refinement is found in the fact that the outer two windows in each group of four are slightly narrower

than the inner two. This variation can be explained by saying that it expresses the width of the piers, which are wider than the mullions, or intermediate stiffeners of the glass, and therefore take up some of the space here. This is an acceptable explanation, but Mies van der Rohe did not always vary windows in this way. This kind of effect is better put down simply to the creative energy of the artist, in this particular design, at this moment of his career, which no explanation can quite capture. In any case, the variation adds zest and vitality to the design and reminds us that we are in the presence of architecture as art rather than mere engineering, however important the construction may have been as a basis for the design. The same architect later designed the two buildings at 900 and 910 Lake Shore Drive.

102 Lake Point Tower. 1968.
East Grand Avenue, east of North Lake Shore Drive.

Architects: Schipporeit-Heinrich Associates; Graham, Anderson, Probst, and White.

The astonishing tower that rises near the base of Navy Pier is first of all a structural masterpiece; its 645-foot height made it the highest reinforced concrete building in the world at the time of its completion, and its flat-slab frame with a shear-wall core in the shape of a triangular prism constitutes a unique structural system in kind and size. The three-lobed shape of the tower was derived from a celebrated skyscraper project that Mies van der Rohe proposed for Berlin in 1921. The young architects who created the Lake Point design were students of Mies at IIT and members of his office staff, and they were the first to adapt the Berlin concept to an executed building. The curving form allowed greater freedom in apartment planning and offered less surface area exposed to direct wind loads than the conventional rectangular prism. The visual impact of these vast, hollowed, and swelling shapes is unparalleled in the building art. The curtain walls of bronze-tinted glass set in a framework of bronze-anodized aluminum produce reflection patterns of vertical ribbons, ranging in color from intense golden sunlight to deep bronze-black shadows. The two-story base structure extending westward from the tower contains the usual public spaces topped by a landscaped park with a lagoon and a swimming pool.

103 John Hancock Center. 1969.
North Michigan Avenue between Chestnut and Delaware streets.

Architects: Skidmore, Owings and Merrill.

Like Marina City, this is a multifunction building: there are shops and businesses on the concourse level and lower floors; twenty-nine floors of office space and forty-eight floors of apartments; and an observatory, two-level restaurant, and radio and television facilities at the top. The tapering form of the 1,105-foot structure, in which all four walls are inclined inward from the vertical, was used only once before in the design of an office building—and then merely to create a sensation. In the case of the Hancock, the form was adopted to provide maximum floor area for public shopping areas at the base, less extensive but still a large floor area at the office levels, and the smallest area for the apartments, insuring an outside exposure for all rooms. By placing the maximum horizontal dimensions at the base and allowing them to diminish steadily toward the top, the designers provided greater stability against wind loads than is offered by a standard rectangular form. The external diagonal braces, each pair extending across eighteen floors, brace the tower against wind loads with less steel than is required in a conventional frame.

The John Hancock's tapering profile is more graceful and soaring than the rectangular, and paradoxically it also gives the impression of maximum stability. The diagonals add visual interest to the pattern of columns and girders by establishing a separate but harmonious geometry that serves to lead the eye from the human scale of the individual windows to the vast technological scale of the whole structure.

104 Time-Life Building. 1970.
541 North Fairbanks Court.

Architects: Harry Weese and Associates.

This well-proportioned building is reinforced concrete with a curtain wall of gold-tinted reflecting glass framed by weathering steel that has now turned a rich, rusty brown. Structural bays are 30 feet square; the building is seven bays long and three bays wide. The thirty-story structure has a high (87-foot) base that contains a 27-foot-high granite lobby and several service floors. The lobby is divided into two levels to accommodate tandem elevators, which were used here for the first time in the United States. A two-story cab carries people in the upper portion to even-numbered floors and those in the lower portion to odd-numbered floors. This reduces elevator shafts 30 percent without decreasing service. The lobby is divided into several smaller areas, creating human-scaled spaces which are so conspicuously missing in most contemporary office buildings.

105 Prentice Women's Hospital and Maternity Center and the Northwestern Institute of Psychiatry. 1975.

333 East Superior Street.

Architects: Bertrand Goldberg Associates.

This dramatic and structurally innovative building serves Northwestern University as both a women's hospital and a psychiatric hospital. The structure consists of a four-story rectilinear base and a seven-story quatrefoil tower. The base is of simple column-and-beam construction and is clad in a curtain wall of metal panels and glass. This portion houses admissions, administrative, and doctors' offices; labor, delivery, and operating rooms; outpatient psychiatric units; and a cafeteria. The tower springs from and is supported by the central core (which contains elevator shafts and stairwells), making this the first structure of its size in which floors and curtain walls are fully cantilevered from a central core. This structural system provides column-free spaces in the tower, where the patients' rooms are located. In plan, the tower consists of two intersecting ovals containing four clusters of rooms radiating out from a central service area. This enables patients to be grouped according to care requirements and also places the nursing station equidistant from every patient's room, making care most efficient.

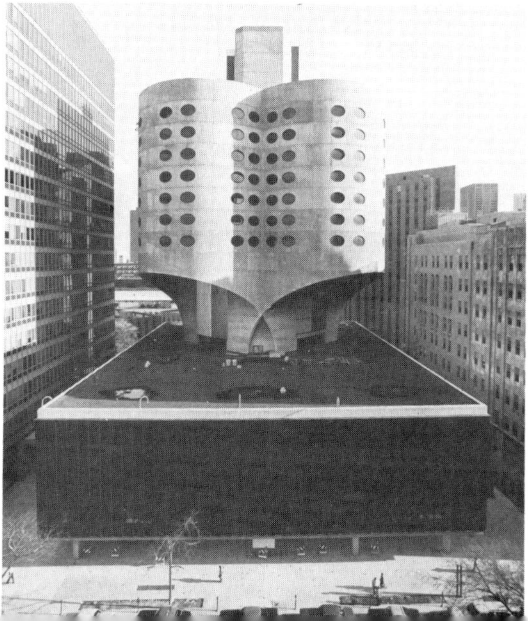

106 Water Tower Place. 1976.
Michigan Avenue, and Chestnut, Seneca, and Pearson streets.

Architects: Loebl, Schlossman, Bennett and Dart; associate architects: C. F. Murphy and Associates.

Although the exterior resembles a huge marble monolith, colorless and fortresslike, the interior is dazzling with its marble, glass, and chrome appointments. The ride up the escalator or, better still, the glass-enclosed elevator can be a spectacular experience.

The twelve-story base contains a vertical shopping mall and offices. At the southeast section is a sixty-two story tower containing a Ritz-Carlton Hotel and luxury condominium apartments.

The mall with seven floors is constructed around a great atrium and five courts. Over 100 stores, shops, theaters, and boutiques are contained within about 610,000 square feet of floor space. The eighth and ninth floors have about 200,000 square feet of office space. The tenth and eleventh floors contain the hotel's health spa facilities and mechanical system, while the twelfth floor is devoted to the hotel lobby and restaurants.

Near West Area

107 St. Patrick's Church. 1854. **NR**
718 West Adams Street.

Architect unknown.

Chicago's oldest surviving church building, St. Patrick's is an example of the Romanesque revival style (often called Norman in the 1850s) characterized by round arches, narrow windows, and broad massive walls. Typical of the style also are the arched "corbel-tables" (thickened horizontal strips of wall carried on masonry projections called "corbels," here connected by small arches against the wall). The small octagonal towers are not ineffective, given the small scale of all the elements—for instance, the narrow arched windows (compare Holy Family Church, No. 109). Originally the center of the facade ended in a gable at the top, and there were no belfry stories or spires on the towers (although they doubtless were intended from the beginning).

108 Jane Addams's Hull House and Dining Hall. 1856. **CL, NR**

800 South Halsted Street.

Architect unknown: house constructed 1856; dining hall, Pond and Pond, architects (1905); restoration and reconstruction, Frazier, Raftery, Orr and Fairbank, architects (1967).

These buildings are all that remain of the most famous social settlement in the United States. In 1856, Charles Hull built this Italianate residence in what was then a suburban area just southwest of downtown Chicago. Hull moved out a dozen years later, and by the 1880s the house was surrounded by factories and tenements. In 1889, Jane Addams and Ellen Gates Starr rented several rooms in the house and started a social settlement to aid the urban poor, particularly the large immigrant population in the immediate vicinity. As the settlement expanded its programs, additional space was needed. The veranda and cupola were removed from the house, and a third floor was added. Gradually, twelve additional structures (including the residents' dining hall that remains), all designed by Irving and Allen Pond, were built around the Hull residence so that the original house was barely visible.

During her years at Hull House, Jane Addams worked to improve the working and living conditions of laborers, immigrants, Negroes, women, children, and the poor. Her efforts greatly influenced the social reform movement throughout the world and earned her the Nobel Peace Prize in 1931. After her death in 1935, the Hull House Association continued her work at the settlement until the early 1960s, when the property was acquired for construction of a new campus of the University of Illinois. The association at that time decided to decentralize its activities throughout the city. With the exception of the dining hall, which was moved about 200 yards from its original site, all the buildings surrounding the original house were demolished. The third-floor addition to the house was removed, the cupola and veranda recreated, and the house restored as a memorial to Jane Addams.

109 Holy Family Church. 1860.

Architect: John M. Van Osdel?

St. Ignatius High School (College). 1869. NR
1076 and 1072 West Roosevelt Road.

Architect unknown.

A great barnlike building of brick, this church follows the Gothic style, as seen in the pointed arches found not only over the large openings but also as small components of the "corbel-tables" (compare No. 107). Alternation of windows and buttresses in the walls of the side aisles results in a simple rhythm of some interest; but throughout the building one is struck most by a self-conscious and artificial use of Gothic details, as in the combination of a pointed arch and a gable in relief over it, found both on the exterior and in the interior. The facade is of painted-over brick; and the interior piers are also of brick but covered with stucco in imitation of stone. The smaller tower is of stone and the larger one of sheet metal.

Various parts of the present church were built at different dates, and several architects were involved, of whom Van Osdel was one. He apparently designed, or carried out from some other architect's design, the original facade and the main body of the church, both finished in 1860; and presumably he also executed the transepts, finished in 1862. In 1866 the facade was torn down and rebuilt, wider and some distance south of its original location, in order to enlarge the church in that direction, the central part being rebuilt exactly as before. The larger tower (designed by Judas Huber) was built in 1874. The adjacent high school (college) is considerably more attractive than the church because of its greater simplicity and directness.

110 Jackson Boulevard District. **CL**
1500 Block of West Jackson Boulevard.

This block of houses typifies the pleasant environment of the Near West Side when that area was a fashionable residential community at the end of the nineteenth century. Ornamental details of the architectural styles popular during the period of the street's development—Italianate, Queen Anne, and Richardsonian Romanesque—abound intact. The most prominent resident of the street was Carter Henry Harrison, who served as mayor of Chicago for five terms beginning in 1879 and lived in a house at Jackson and Ashland which has since been demolished. Benjamin F. Ferguson, a benefactor of the Art Institute, lived at 1501 Jackson Boulevard for a time.

111 Schoenhofen Brewery Building. 1902. NR
West 18th Street and Canalport (NE corner).

Architects: Richard E. Schmidt; Hugh Garden.

An interesting example of the work of the group of architects who were developing a nonhistorical approach at the beginning of the century, this building demonstrates a fine appreciation of the qualities of brick and considerable inventiveness in attaining accents or emphases by the way it is laid. Although Schmidt was the commissioned architect, the design was apparently made by Hugh Garden, who was occasionally retained by Schmidt for a given design prior to 1906, the year they formed a partnership.

112 University of Illinois at Chicago Circle. 1965–.
Harrison and Halsted streets.

Architects: Skidmore, Owings and Merrill; C. F. Murphy Associates; A. Epstein and Sons.

The campus is planned around a lecture center and a great court. The lecture center contains lecture halls in six buildings which share a common roof. This roof forms the great court, approached by

elevated express walkways connecting it with major campus buildings, and containing an outdoor amphitheater. The staff and administration building is a twenty-eight-story skyscraper, the others are lower. All are arranged in accord with a master plan that provides for flow of traffic within and to the campus and that seeks not only to relate the buildings in a coherent design but to create a campus in harmony with its urban environment.

113 **Rush University Academic Facility. 1976.**
600 South Paulina Street.

Architects: Metz, Train, Olson and Youngren

Located on a narrow site traversed by an elevated track, this structure rests on and is cantilevered out from three-story (43-foot) columns, which enables it to span the tracks and increases its width from 90 to 120 feet. At the north, the building angles across Harrison Street to connect with Rush–Presbyterian–St. Luke's Hospital. It also connects with a professional building to the west and a health care facility for the elderly at the south, functioning as an integral part of the hospital complex and providing for the interconnection of these buildings. Because future expansion was an essential part of the design program, the structure was built so that seven additional floors can be added to the top and another suspended from the bottom, with two additional floors built up from the ground if necessary. To provide a sound barrier between the trains and the building, a highly reflective roof above the tracks bounces noise onto side walls composed of sand-filled concrete blocks with sound-absorptive panels. The building is innovative in its use of interstitial space, which is a deep space between floors that accommodates ducts, wires, and pipes. Because this space is easily accessible, maintenance or future adaptation to new mechanical systems can be accomplished efficiently and relatively inexpensively. The cantilevered structure required a lightweight cladding, so a curtain wall of light natural aluminum and solar gray glass was used. The horizontal bands of windows and sleek surface treatment are reminiscent of the Art Moderne style of the 1930s.

114 Illinois Regional Library for the Blind and Physically Handicapped. 1978.
1055 West Roosevelt Road.

Architect: Stanley Tigerman as consultant to Jerome R. Butler, Jr., City Architect.

This witty and colorful building houses a state distribution center for Braille library materials, a city-wide library for the blind and physically handicapped, and, on the second floor, a local branch of the Chicago Public Library. Circulation areas of the interior are marked by linear plans and built-in furnishings which are easily memorized so that blind users can maneuver conveniently. Directly inside the diagonal west wall is the circulation corridor which is defined by a long curving counter. The counter curves inward at each of four service desks so that a user can there move out of the main aisle. The curving corridor is reflected on the exterior by a whimsical undulating window set into the con-

crete wall. The lowest part of the window is the right height for someone in a wheelchair, and the higher points are opposite the service desks so that library personnel can see out.

Paradoxes appear throughout the design. The lightweight baked enamel panels that cover most of the structure are infrequently broken by small windows, making them seem heavy. On the other hand, the structural concrete wall is broken by the long undulating window, making it seem light. Because of a tri-level arrangement of the stacks, the smaller exterior elements are three stories high, and the larger elements are only two stories. The structure is brightly colored, although it is meant to serve the blind—all structural parts are painted yellow; mechanical ducts and electrical and plumbing conduits are blue; and the metal wall panels are red. The bright colors offer a vivid contrast to the drab surrounding and enliven a structure that serves a very serious purpose.

Near South Area

115 **Prairie Avenue Historic District.** **NR**

South Prairie Avenue between 18th and 20th streets.

From the 1870s through the remainder of the nineteenth century, many of Chicago's prominent merchants, manufacturers, and businessmen—including Marshall Field, George M. Pullman, and John J. Glessner—lived in imposing residences along Prairie Avenue. Later the area declined, and most of the grand houses were demolished. Those that remain portray the elegance of that era, and form the nucleus of the Prairie Avenue Historic District created by the Chicago Architecture Foundation and the City of Chicago. The cornerstone of the district is the Glessner House (No. 118). Directly across the street is the William W. Kimball House, designed by Solon S. Beman and built in 1892. It is Chicago's best remaining example of the French chateau style, and displays the steeply sloped roofs, slender chimneys with corbeled tops, and copper-clad finials characteristic of that style. To the south, at 1811 South Prairie, is the Coleman House, a Romanesque structure demonstrating Richardson's influence. Designed by Cobb and Frost, it was built around 1886. The earliest house remaining on Prairie Avenue is the Elbridge Keith House, built in the early 1870s in an Italianate style. The houses here, along with the architectural fragment park planned for the open space, constitute an outdoor museum of urban change.

116 Henry B. Clarke House. 1836. CL, NR
1855 South Indiana Avenue.

Architect: unknown.

Sometimes known as the Widow Clarke House, this is the oldest building still standing in Chicago. Its portico, or porch, has been removed, as have the original tall window shutters. But the proportions, the placing of the windows, and even the towerlike cupola on top remain. The influence of classical models is seen in the low-pitched gable on the front, as well as in the simple moldings. The spaciousness of the first elegant homes of the city is suggested by the triple-sashed windows, which tell of the high-ceilinged rooms within.

The house was moved from its original site shortly after the Chicago Fire of 1871. For many years it stood at 45th Street and Wabash Avenue and served as a meeting hall for a church. It has now been returned to approximately its original site as part of the Prairie Avenue District.

117 Second Presbyterian Church. 1874. CL, NR
1936 South Michigan Avenue.

Architect: James Renwick; remodeled by Howard Van Doren Shaw (1901).

James Renwick, the New York architect who designed this church, was one of the foremost practitioners of the Gothic revival style. After a fire in 1900, Howard Van Doren Shaw designed a new interior and modified the exterior. Shaw replaced the traditional pointed arch clerestory windows with simple rectangular ones, replaced the rose window above the entrance with an ogee-shaped window, and lowered the ridge of the roof. Perhaps the most noteworthy feature of the church is its windows. Seven of these art glass windows, including the one over the Michigan Avenue entrance, were executed by the Tiffany Company. Two small art glass windows in the vestibule were designed by the English Pre-Raphaelite Edward Burne-Jones and executed by William Morris. The murals were designed by Frederick Clay Bartlett, a Chicago artist whose work is incorporated into the Bartlett Gymnasium at the University of Chicago and who donated the Birch-Bartlett collection at the Art Institute of Chicago. For many years, this church served a wealthy congregation that included many residents of Prairie Avenue as well as Mrs. Abraham Lincoln and her son Robert Todd Lincoln.

118 Glessner House. 1886. CL, NR
1800 South Prairie Avenue.

Architect: H. H. Richardson.

A particularly well-planned residence for an urban site, the house encloses a private courtyard, and the principal family rooms turn away from the city streets and face the quiet court. The superb handling of rugged masonry forms, particularly the powerful arch on the 18th Street facade, and the effective ornament make this one of Richardson's finest works. It is the only remaining building in Chicago designed by this important American architect. Since 1966, the house has been owned by the Chicago Architecture Foundation, which has restored some rooms and adapted others for contemporary use.

119 R. R. Donnelley and Sons Company Building. 1912.

350 East 22d Street

Architect: Howard Van Doren Shaw (1912, 1917, 1924); Charles Z. Klauder (1931).

When the Donnelley Company outgrew its printing plant on Plymouth Court (No. 23), the same architect was commissioned to design this new plant. Like its predecessor, it is an excellent industrial building. In both, Shaw employed traditional forms in highly original ways. Here the facade is more straightforward: broad piers define wide rectangular bays, and carefully proportioned spandrels and windows create a uniform rhythm from bottom to top. Gothic elements are employed extensively, from the buttressed corner tower to the limestone trim. The ornament incorporates emblems of early printers. Altogether, this is a vigorous and nicely detailed building that expresses its industrial purpose.

120 Field Museum of Natural History. 1912. NR
South Lake Shore Drive at East Roosevelt Road.

Architects: D. H. Burnham and Company (until 1912); Graham, Burnham and Company (1912–17); Graham, Anderson, Probst and White (1917–20); renovation by Harry Weese and Associates (completed 1978).

The idea for the Field Museum of Natural History grew out of planning for the World's Columbian Exposition of 1893. Many of the fair's backers believed that the objects being collected for display at the fair should have a permanent home in Chicago after its conclusion. An initial gift of $1 million from Marshall Field helped secure use of the Palace of Fine Arts at the fair (today the Museum of Science and Industry, see No. 141), and the museum's early collection was housed there until 1920. A bequest of another $8 million in Field's will enabled the museum to build its present home. Working drawings for the building were completed in 1906, but construction did not begin until 1915. Beginning in 1920, the collection was moved from Jackson Park, and the museum opened in 1921. The building was designed in the classical style of the fair, and employs several motifs—the caryatids, for example—of the Erechtheion on the Acropolis. The building consists of a great central hall that rises to a height of 76 feet and is flanked at each side by seven three-story transverse halls. These transverse halls are joined at the east and west ends by long halls parallel to the central hall. The central hall—named Stanley Field Hall after Field's nephew, who was the museum's president for over fifty years—is one of the most impressive monumental interior spaces in Chicago. The museum's siting is superb, and the vista from the top of its broad north steps is one of the city's finest.

121 Park Buildings, Fuller Park. 1915.
45th Street and South Princeton Avenue.

Architect: Edward H. Bennett.

These buildings are interesting for the inventive use of concrete for texture and pattern, as in the waffle-like areas, or for forms inspired by classical architecture but carried out in concrete, as in the pilasters, or decorative strips, at the sides of the large windows. The planning is clear and spacious. Note the way the niches enliven the space of the entrance vestibule of the main building. The links connecting the gymnasiums to the main building have been remodeled, the roofs of each link having had originally a small gable echoing those on the front of the main building.

122 John G. Shedd Aquarium. 1929.
South Lake Shore Drive at East Roosevelt Road.

Architects: Graham, Anderson, Probst and White.

The entrance portico of the aquarium is the gabled facade of a Doric temple. The actual plan of the main building is a Greek cross, but because the inner corners of the cross are filled in, the resulting shape is more like an octagon with blunt wings extending along the east-west and north-south lines. The central rotunda is surmounted by a low octagonal tower roofed by a pyramidal skylight. The soft diffused light that descends through this skylight onto the circular pool and vine-covered island below forms one of the pleasing features of the aquarium. The smooth exterior walls of Georgia marble sheathing are punctuated by narrow windows on the diagonal sides of the enclosures, behind which the working areas are located. The white-walled building was clearly designed to express the bright translucency of shells and coral. This quality and the simplified classical detail make it appropriate both to its sparkling lakeshore setting and to the dim aqueous luminosity of its interior.

123 Max Adler Planetarium. 1930.
East end of Achsah Bond.

Architect: Ernest Grunsfeld; 1973 extension: C. F. Murphy and Associates.

This planetarium building, the first erected in the United States, is a design of classic simplicity and purity. The main structure is basically a regular twelve-sided figure developed into three concentric enclosures rising in tiers as they contract in diameter. The innermost of the three contains the cylindrical planetarium chamber and is surmounted by a lead-sheathed hemispherical dome from which hangs an inner dome that serves as a projection screen. The main building volume is sheathed in polished red and black granite, its ornamentation reduced chiefly to narrow fluting at the corners of the polygons. The harmony of the geometric forms, the rich material of the exterior covering, and the elevation of the building well above the level of the drive that encircles it gives the Adler Planetarium an elegance and dignity that are enhanced by its very simplicity. The setting is without parallel among American cities—the view from the site, which lies far out in the lake at the end of a long peninsula, includes Chicago Harbor and behind it one of the greatest urban vistas in the world.

An addition below grade was designed by C. F. Murphy and Associates and opened in 1973, more than doubling the floor space of the planetarium. The addition contains the main entrance, exhibit space, library, and a theater.

124 On Leong Chinese Merchants Association. 1930.
2216 South Wentworth Avenue.

Architects: Michaelsen and Rognstad.

This brick- and terra-cotta-clad structure was built as the headquarters of a Chinese-American businessman's association that dates from the early twentieth century. The two fanciful pagodas, the elaborately canopied entrance, the upper arcades, and the colorful ornament are the primary elements of the design. This building and the entrance arch to the north reflect ethnic pride and serve as an appropriate entrance to Chicago's Chinatown.

125 Illinois Institute of Technology Campus. 1942–58.

South State Street, 31st to 35th Streets.

Architects: Mies van der Rohe; Friedman, Alschuler and Sincere; Holabird and Root; Pace Associates.

Aside from the individual merit of some buildings, the campus is of great interest for the grouping of a number of structures by one of the masters of modern architecture. The buildings are related so as to suggest courts or quadrangles, but these are never completely closed, one such suggested space overlapping or opening into another, usually asymmetrically. This results in fascinating and varying visual relationships and is highly expressive of a modern ideal, the combination of freedom and order. Of particular interest among the buildings designed by Mies are the Alumni Memorial Building, 1946 (especially for the detailing, as at the corners); the Chapel, 1952; and Crown Hall, 1956. The main floor of the last, which houses the Institute's department of architecture, is a notable expression of freedom of space.

126 McCormick Place. 1970.
South Lake Shore Drive at 23d Street.

Architects: C. F. Murphy and Associates.

An earlier metropolitan exposition building, named McCormick Place after Robert R. McCormick of the *Chicago Tribune,* was destroyed by fire on January 16, 1967. Its replacement, which was designed and redesigned several times before an adequate solution was found, represents an enormous architectural improvement over the original, although its setting in a lakefront recreational area is questionable. The problem was to produce a building with greatly expanded floor space that could be erected on the foundations of its predecessor. The

solution was to introduce a two-level exposition area in the north portion of the enclosure, a 5,000-seat theater in the south, and a broad pedestrian mall between the two, the entire complex placed under a single roof measuring 19 acres in area. The roof is carried on a two-way system of deep trusses supported in turn by four rows of columns spaced 150 feet on centers. The roof is cantilevered on all four sides beyond the walls of the enclosed areas. The uninterrupted planes of glass extending from the main floor level to the underside of the roof frame and the exposed trusswork combine qualities of lightness and delicacy with immense horizontal dimensions. It is a fine example of the elegance and strength of steel construction.

Far North Area

127 Getty Tomb. Graceland Cemetery. 1890. **CL, NR**
4001 North Clark Street.

Architect: Louis H. Sullivan.

Sullivan designed this simple cubic form with exquisite ornament as an appropriately serene and feminine tomb for the wife of a Chicago lumber merchant. The ornament cut into the stone is remarkable for the way in which an apparently routine geometrical motif, a spokelike figure inside an octagon, becomes, when repeated, a decoration of the greatest delicacy, like an openwork veil drawn over the solid stone. The bronze doors contain some of Sullivan's finest ornament, with the spoke motif of the stone ornament above subtly echoed within the rich floral design. The Getty Tomb has been called "a requiem for the dead, an inspiration to the living."

128 Hutchinson Street District. CL
Hutchinson Street between Marine Drive and Hazel Street.

These two blocks contain a unique concentration of houses designed by George Maher (see also Magerstadt House, No. 143). Maher is frequently classified as a Prairie School architect, although his designs are highly eclectic and employ forms borrowed from various architectural idioms. His houses on Hutchinson Street amply demonstrate this. The first house Maher designed here was built in 1894 at the northeast corner of Hutchinson and Hazel. It is a picturesque Queen Anne house with a lively profusion of projecting bays, porches, and turret; a complex pattern of roofs with ornamented gables; and a variety of different building materials. Maher's next house on Hutchinson Street was built in 1904 at 826. Its broad horizontal lines and formal composition demonstrate the influence of Frank Lloyd Wright's early work (for example, the Charnley House, No. 79, and the Winslow House in River Forest, No. 161). The period between 1905 and 1910, during which he designed the house at 839 Hutchinson Street, saw Maher experimenting with forms then being used by certain European architects. The irregular arrangement of windows in a broad wall plane seen here is an example. Maher's most impressive design on the street is the house built in 1913 at 817. It displays a Prairie School horizontality, has long bands of windows, and demonstrates Maher's "motif-rhythm theory," which calls for the repetition of a single decorative element throughout a design to create unity. Here, the geometric pattern of the windows is echoed on the porch balustrade. The house at 750 Hutchinson was also designed by Maher and has a front door set into a stone frame that is reminiscent of the design of Louis Sullivan's Wainwright Tomb in St. Louis. The Hutchinson Street District contains several other excellent houses built around the turn of the century. The nicely massed and finely detailed house at 4234 Hazel Street, built in 1904, was designed by William Drummond for the office of Richard Schmidt. Both of these architects are grouped with the Prairie School.

129 Alta Vista Terrace District. **CL, NR**
1900–1904.

One-block-long street, running north-south, located at 3800 N. 1050 W.

Architect: Possibly J. C. Brompton.

Alta Vista Terrace is composed of forty masonry row houses, twenty on each side of the block-long street, which runs from Grace Street on the south to Byron Street on the north. Each row house is situated on a lot approximately 24 feet wide and 40 feet deep with brick party walls, 18 inches thick, between them. This gives a continuous facade on each side of the terrace of approximately 480 feet. The buildings are particularly noteworthy for their unity of scale.

The facades reflect adaptations of various architectural styles, including the Gothic and late Renaissance revivals and even—in a later modification of one front—false half-timbering. In what were originally the twenty different Roman-brick facades of the forty houses are to be found such divergent architectural motifs as Doric and Ionic wood pilasters, flamboyant Gothic arches, Palladian windows, stained- and leaded-glass fanlights, bay and bow windows, sheet-metal cornices at roof levels, and a wealth of moldings, brackets, dentils, festoons, and other classic details.

130 Carl Schurz High School. 1909.

Milwaukee Avenue at Addison Street.

Architect: Dwight H. Perkins.

This school building is a dramatic composition of rising verticals in the walls, suddenly stopped by the deep overhangs of high-pitched roofs set at varying levels. A very strong string course at the top of the first floor echoes the roof line. The building is well sited with sufficient space around it for it to be seen clearly.

131 **Grover Cleveland Elementary School. 1910.**
350 North Albany Street.

Architect: Dwight H. Perkins.

Another example of the work of Perkins, who to some degree specialized in school architecture, this school is less varied and dramatic than his Carl Schurz School (No. 130). It has a strong and severe design, the chief forms emphasized by borders of contrasting brick. The piers terminate in an interesting capital block, which makes an effective transition to the wall above. (By a curious optical illusion these piers seem wider at the second and third stories than at the first, perhaps because of their lighter color.)

132 The Emil Bach House. 1915. **CL**
7415 North Sheridan Road.

Architect: Frank Lloyd Wright.

Although strictly urban in size and character, the Emil Bach House has many of the characteristics of Wright's earlier Prairie houses. By stressing the horizontal axis, the house is related to the prairie and firmly rooted in the earth. The plan was determined by a rectangular grid, which became the basis for this small-scale, compact rectangular building. The surrounding high-rise buildings, instead of dwarfing the house, actually call attention to the unique semicubist design of its facade. This was one of Wright's last small urban commissions and is one of the few Frank Lloyd Wright houses in the city of Chicago.

133 Immaculata High School. 1922. NR
600 West Irving Park Road.

Architect: Barry Byrne.

The architect of this school, an early and important student of Frank Lloyd Wright, studied at Wright's Oak Park studio from 1902 until 1908. The building is L-shaped in plan, with the hollow of the L facing southwest on Irving Park Road. The walls are brown tapestry brick with limestone trim, and the roof is red tile with low, unusually shaped, copper-clad dormers. Windows are banked vertically under pointed arches. The terra-cotta canopy and statue of the Virgin at the front entrance are the work of Alfonso Ianelli, who worked frequently with Byrne and had also worked with Wright, designing, for example, the sculpture at Wright's Midway Gardens (demolished 1929).

134 Krause Music Store. 1922. **CL**

4611 North Lincoln Avenue.

Architects: Louis H. Sullivan and William C. Presto. (Now the Arntzen-Coleman Company).

This small store was designed by a minor architect, but its facade design was the last commission received by Louis Sullivan. Certain elements of the facade—the restrained ornament in the recessed entryway and the sensitive patterning of the upper wall—are typical of Sullivan's finest work. On the other hand, the three large ornamental forms up and down the center line of the facade seem hung on rather than integrated with the design as a whole. They overwhelm the little facade, which is far too short to carry such an emphatic central emphasis.

135 Chicago O'Hare International Airport. 1963.
Northwest Far City Limits.

Architects: Naess and Murphy.

An example of the world-wide transportation terminal of the present day: a large airport, connected with the downtown area by a modern high-speed

artery, the John F. Kennedy (Northwest) Expressway. The large-scale planning is noteworthy, especially in the arrangement of the various terminals. a hotel, the fields, hangars, maintenance areas, and levels of roadway. The spreading U-shaped supports of the latter are very handsome pieces of engineering architecture.

Far South Area

136 Kenwood District. CL, NR

Between East 47th and East 51st streets, South Blackstone Avenue and South Drexel Boulevard.

Kenwood developed as a comfortable suburb from 1856, when Dr. John A. Kennicott built the first house in the community, to 1889, when it was annexed to the City of Chicago. During the three decades following its annexation, many wealthy Kenwood residents commissioned some of the city's most prominent architects to design large houses set on spacious lots. Kenwood acquired the character of a late-nineteenth-century suburban community, a character that it preserves today.

The earliest surviving residences, including the house at 4812 Woodlawn, are Italianate in style and were built when Kenwood was a sparsely settled suburban area in the 1870s. During the 1880s, a large number of Queen Anne and Shingle-style houses were built in the area. Both of these styles are characterized by an irregularity of plan and massing. Queen Anne houses generally display a lively variety of building materials of different colors and textures, while Shingle-style houses are sheathed in horizontal bands of shingles. A large concentration of these houses is found on Kimbark Avenue between 47th and 49th streets.

During the 1890s, historical revival styles prevailed in Kenwood. Noteworthy examples include

the Tudor revival house at 4815 Woodlawn designed by Howard Van Doren Shaw and built in 1910, the Georgian revival house at 4858 Dorchester Avenue designed by the firm of Handy and Cady and built in 1897, and the Renaissance revival house at 4900 Ellis Avenue designed by Horatio Wilson and Benjamin Marshall and built in 1899. In 1892, Frank Lloyd Wright designed a Colonial revival house for George Blossom at 4858 Kenwood Avenue. During the following decade, Wright developed his distinctive Prairie School style characterized by broad horizontal lines, and in 1907 he designed a Prairie-style carriage house for the Blossoms. These two adjacent structures, separated by fifteen years in Wright's career, provide a unique perspective on the development of his architecture.

Wright exerted a tremendous influence on many of his Midwestern contemporaries, and a few of these Prairie School architects designed homes in Kenwood. The finest is the Ernest J. Magerstadt House (No. 143), designed by George Maher. The Julius Rosenwald House at 4901 Ellis Avenue, designed by George C. Nimmons in 1899, also displays elements of the Prairie style.

The major period of Kenwood's development ended with the start of the Depression in 1929. The deterioration of the areas to the north and west threatened the community's future during the early 1950s. Today, however, Kenwood is a well-preserved neighborhood that retains a unique suburban character.

137 South Pullman District. 1880–1894. CL, NR

South Cottage Grove Avenue to South Langely Avenue between East 111th and East 11th streets.

Architect: S. S. Beman.

The town of Pullman was built by the Pullman Company to accommodate its manufacturing activities and provide housing for its employees; as such it was America's first completely planned company town. The buildings were designed by Beman and the public spaces laid out by landscape architect Nathan Barrett. Much renovation and restoration activity has taken place in the community, and the character of the original town has been preserved. Consequently, Pullman is interesting as an example of the contemporary ideas on town planning. One of the most prominent buildings in the community is the Queen Anne–style Hotel Florence, with its picturesque profusion of roofs, dormers, and gables.

138 St. Gabriel's Church. 1887.
4501 South Lowe.

Architects: Burnham and Root.

This building is remarkable in the bold, broad massing of the chief elements, including the chapels at the back. The effect of breadth and strength is emphasized by the subtle batter (the inward slope of the wall as it rises) which is nicely worked out in the brick at the foot of the walls. The tower has been lowered by the removal of a section that was just below the present top story, and the latter has been rebuilt in line with the lower stories, whereas it originally projected beyond them. The tower has thus lost in force as well as in height. The present entrance porch has been added, and there are minor changes, as in the buttresses. The interior maintains its original breadth and spaciousness because of the broad vaulted shapes of the ceiling, although there has been some remodeling, especially in the northern part. Despite changes, the building still has a degree of individuality and character recalling the Rookery (No. 8), by the same architects.

139 University of Chicago Campus. 1891–.

Between Blackstone and Cottage Grove avenues, and East 55th and East 60th streets.

This is one of the finest campus designs in the country, in large part because a unified plan was conceived at the very beginning and basically adhered to during the first four decades of the university's growth; later buildings have been consistently designed to be compatible in material and/or scale to the earlier structures. Founded in 1891 with a substantial endowment from John D. Rockefeller, the university early commissioned Henry Ives Cobb to design the campus and its buildings. Cobb based his design on the campuses of major English universities and chose Tudor Gothic as the architectural style. Blue Bedford limestone was chosen as the basic building material. The quadrangles occupy the four-block area between 57th and 59th streets from University to Ellis avenues. A broad central space

bisects this area along the east-west axis. To the north and south, two quadrangles are defined and separated by a court that opens onto the central space. Many of the early buildings of this composition were designed by Cobb himself. After the turn of the century, Shepley, Rutan and Coolidge became the campus architects. This Boston firm was successsor to the office of Henry Hobson Richardson, and also designed Chicago's Art Institute (No. 14) and Public Library (No. 88). They followed Cobb's design and had largely defined the present configuration of the quadrangles by 1915. After that, commissions for individual buildings went to different architects. Holabird and Roche, the most prolific architects of the Chicago School, were commissioned to design Rosenwald Hall, built in 1915, and produced an excellent essay in the Gothic style. Howard Van Doren Shaw, who frequently employed traditional forms in original ways, designed the Quadrangle Club, built in 1921. The intimate Bond Chapel, built in 1926, was the design of Coolidge and Hodgson (successor to

Shepley, Rutan and Coolidge), who did many campus buildings during the 1920s. The Depression and Second World War interrupted building activity, and by the time it resumed, academic imitation of historical style had given way to designs that respect the scale and materials of the original campus.

The Administration Building of 1948, designed by Holabird, Root and Burgee, is a nondescript building distinguished by its compatibility with its surroundings; anything else on so prominent a site would have been disastrous. Several major contemporary architects are represented on the campus. The buildings include Eero Saarinen's Woodward Court residence hall of 1958 and his law school complex of 1960 on the south side of the Midway. The angled glass walls of the law school library dominate that composition, which also consists of a low classroom wing and an auditorium structure in the shape of an eight-pointed star. Ludwig Mies van der Rohe is represented by his low, pavilionlike Social Service Administration Building of 1964. The Gothic towers of the original buildings are

echoed in I. W. Colburn's Henry Hinds Laboratory for the Geophysical Sciences of 1969 (done in collaboration with J. Lee Jones) and his Cummings Life Science Center of 1973 (in collaboration with Schmidt, Garden and Erickson and Harold H. Hellman, University Architect). Another contemporary reflection of the Gothic influence is Skidmore, Owings and Merrill's Joseph Regenstein Library of 1970. Here Gothic verticality is subtly echoed in the vertical bands of limestone that animate the facade and in the narrow slotlike windows.

140 Rockefeller Memorial Chapel. 1928.
59th Street at Woodlawn Avenue.

Architect: Bertram G. Goodhue.

Rockefeller Chapel is an impressive example of the later Gothic revival by one of its leading practitioners in the United States. Its massive and solid character contrasts with the lighter quality of the Fourth Presbyterian Church (No. 91) by Goodhue's former partner, Ralph A. Cram.

141 Museum of Science and Industry. 1893.
South Lake Shore Drive at East 57th Street.

Architects: Charles B. Atwood of D. H. Burnham and Company (1893); Graham, Anderson, Probst and White (1929, 1933, 1937, 1940).

Built as a temporary structure to house the Palace of Fine Arts at the World's Columbian Exposition of 1893, this building reflects the classical revival styles that prevailed at the fair. The enormous caryatids that support the pedimented porches are based on those at the Erechtheion on the Acropolis, while other elements of the design derive from the Parthenon. Some features, such as the domes, derive from Roman precedents. Charles B. Atwood, the architect of this structure which is so firmly based on classical precedent, would only a year later design the Reliance Building (No. 20), the most technically advanced structure of its day.

After the Columbian Exposition closed, this building housed the collections of the Field Museum of Natural History until 1920, when a new Field Museum was completed at the south end of Grant Park (No. 120). This building remained empty and deteriorated badly until the mid-1920s, when Julius Rosenwald, president of Sears, Roebuck and Company, proposed that the structure be rehabilitated for use as a museum of science and technology and contributed a generous endowment. Rosenwald had earlier visited the Deutsches Museum in Munich, the first scientific and technical museum in the world, and decided that Chicago should have an equivalent institution. The major feature that had impressed Rosenwald, and that distinguishes the Museum of Science and Industry today, was the large number of exhibits that could actually be operated by spectators.

142 Heller House. 1897. CL, NR
5132 South Woodlawn Avenue.

Architect: Frank Lloyd Wright.

This notable example of Wright's work at this time is still quite blocklike and closed up below, like many of his earlier houses, but it is more open on the upper floor and shows a more interesting silhouette than the Charnley House (No. 79). The lightening and opening of the upper part foreshadows Wright's later designs. The molded plaster frieze at the top is by sculptor Richard Bock.

143 **Magerstadt House. 1906.**

4930 South Greenwood Avenue.

Architect: George W. Maher.

The Magerstadt House was designed by one of the architects who were contemporaries of and influenced by Frank Lloyd Wright. Very shallow brick, with subtle emphasis by projection here and there, is used in a design which consistently emphasizes a more massive quality than is found in Wright's contemporary houses. Perhaps, too, there is more obvious recollection of other styles; the profile of the cornice of the porch and the small rectangular blocks, or "dentils," under it remind one of classical forms, and the foliate ornament on the capitals of the columns perhaps recalls the Art Nouveau decoration at the turn of the century. The long plan and the entrance at the side of the city lot will be found in Wright's Robie House (No. 144); however, the frame around the entrance is more massive and less integrated with the rest of the building than in Wright's famous work.

144 Robie House. 1909. **CL, NR**

5757 South Woodlawn Avenue.

Architect: Frank Lloyd Wright.

One of the most famous houses in the world, Robie House shows the perfected type of the so-called Prairie House, adapted here to a narrow city lot. In its own right it must rate as one of the most

brilliant designs in the history of architecture. The strong horizontal emphasis created by long limestone sills and the broad overhanging roofs were said by Wright to reflect the lines of the Midwestern prairie—hence the term "Prairie School." Interior spaces are organized around the great hearth and extend outward to further elongate the overall form.

145 South Shore Country Club. 1916. **NR**
South Shore Drive and East 71st Street.

Architect: Marshall and Fox.

Incorporated in 1906 as a suburban club in an area then largely undeveloped, the South Shore Country Club grew and prospered as a residential community developed around it in the early years of this century. Membership dwindled as the community changed in the 1960s, and in 1974 the club was sold to the Chicago Park District. The original clubhouse, modeled after one in Mexico City, was built in 1906, was moved closer to the lake when the present structure was built in 1916, and was demolished in 1975. The present clubhouse has a complex silhouette with towers, wings, and projecting colonnades. The facades are rather plain, the walls are covered with cement stucco reminiscent of Mediterranean architecture, and the broad roofs are shingled with clay tiles. The tall windows of the ground floor reflect the grand spaces within and provide those spaces with a commanding view of the lake and the club grounds.

146 University Building. 1937.
5551 South University Avenue.

Architects: George F. and William Keck.

The glass brick and external Venetian blinds of this small, modern-style apartment building seemed "modernistic" in 1937, but today the dominant effect is of quiet design in simple forms carried out in a pleasant red brick.

147 Promontory Apartments. 1949.
5530 South Shore Drive.

Architects: Mies van der Rohe; Pace Associates; Holsman, Holsman and Klekamp.

This building is typical of the postwar trend toward simple style, emphasis on structure, and care in planning, for both cost and efficiency. Here light-colored brick panels and aluminum window frames are set into a reinforced concrete frame, the frame being emphasized by the projection of the columns. The columns are stepped back on the outside at the sixth, eleventh, and sixteenth stories because of the greater load on the lower parts; they are scored, but in this case at every story, in order to soften the effect of the steps by integrating them with a design element. The concrete is "self-finished," not covered with some other material, thus contributing to the simplicity and directness seen throughout.

148 Atrium Houses. 1961.
1370 East Madison Park.

Architect: Y. C. Wong.

These reticent houses are closed up on the outside, opening to an interior court, or "atrium." The exterior walls are of a subdued light tan brick, without decoration or relief, the headers at every sixth course making a scarcely noticeable variation. There is no cornice, only a simple beam at the top of the wall; an extremely modest doorstep leads to the tall simple door openings. Here the architecture quietly but distinctly says "Private."

149 Lutheran School of Theology. 1967.
55th Street at Greenwood Avenue.

Architects: The Perkins and Will Partnership.

The three buildings that comprise the school are joined at their inner corners and arranged in a U-shaped plan with a landscaped court in the enclosed area. The novel structural system is exploited for maximum aesthetic effect: the two-story upper part of any one block, housing classrooms and offices, is lifted a full story above ground by four squat piers that carry the massive supporting girders. The light metal framework of mullions and spandrel panels combined with extensive cantilevers makes the main enclosures appear to be lightly poised on their sturdy underpinnings. The steel rocker bearings at the top of the piers heighten this visual effect.

Suburban Areas

150 Willits House. 1902.
1145 Sheridan Road, Highland Park.

Architect: Frank Lloyd Wright.

One of the earliest and most successful of the large Prairie houses was the Ward W. Willits house, built in 1902. The cruciform plan is basic to literally dozens of houses that followed, designed by Wright and also by members of his school.

A huge multiple fireplace forms the core of the design with the remainder of the house surrounding it. The major rooms have windows on three sides, and circulation is extraordinarily well planned. Sleeping rooms on the second floor are similarly grouped around the central fireplace core. A gardener's cottage on the same site, also by Wright, has been remodeled as a separate residence.

151 Glasner House. 1905.
850 Sheridan Road, Glencoe.

Architect: Frank Lloyd Wright.

This interesting house, with its horizontal board-and-batten siding, was designed by Wright in 1904 and built in the following year. It has an asymmetrical plan around a long central axis with the primary living areas on the top floor. The lower level contains bedrooms as well as a large studio and a garage.

The site, on the edge of a deep ravine, is heavily overgrown with vegetation, obscuring the view except during the winter months.

152 Temple of North Shore Congregation Israel. 1963.

1185 Sheridan Road, Glencoe.

Architect: Minoru Yamasaki.

The entire complex includes the temple proper, offices, facilities for social events, classrooms for the synagogue school, and the covered interconnecting passageways. The temple is the dominant structure and the chief object of architectural interest. The interior space is enclosed by means of unique structural forms which could be fully comprehended only during the construction of the building. Each one combines both column and roof slab in a single continuous element of reinforced concrete, rising from a thin stemlike form at the base and opening gradually into a broad leaflike cantilever at the top. The two rows of these cantilevers, one on either side of the central longitudinal axis, constitute the roof of the tabernacle. The space between any pair of "stems" is filled with a thin flat slab of concrete bordered by amber glass. Each end of the tabernacle is closed by still another leaflike form—in this case a broad slab with a central rib from which two sets of veins curve outward and downward. Unfortunately, the architect elected to cover all parts of the interior of the building with a creamy white paint that softens and blurs the tense and dynamic structural forms to the point where they nearly melt away.

153 Crow Island School. 1940.
1112 Willow, Winnetka.

Architects: Eliel and Eero Saarinen; Perkins, Wheeler and Will.

This pleasingly scaled elementary school in a spacious and leafy suburban setting was one of the first to revive a modern scholastic architecture, which was originally created by Dwight Perkins in Chicago in 1905–10. The local board of education wanted a school that would answer the emotional and intellectual needs of children and would fit their physical scale. The aim was to make the school environment as pleasant and comfortable as possible, so that it might become a positive tool in enhancing the learning process. The architects began with the design of a single classroom, a self-contained prototype that might be used with suitable variations for all age groups. The ultimate design then became a matter of multiplying these units along three wings extending from a central section devoted to common facilities. The classrooms project outward in subsidiary wings from the corridors, each pair of rooms enclosing its associated outdoor play space. The warm color and pleasant texture of brick and wood, the glazed ceramic sculpture set at intervals in the exterior walls, and the delightful scale redeem an otherwise excessively sober design.

154 Baha'i House of Worship. 1953. NR
Sheridan Road at Linden Avenue, Wilmette.

Architect: Louis Bourgeois.

Rising 191 feet from the ground floor to its pinnacle, the temple contains four stories of lace-like reinforced concrete, with tall windows and elaborate carvings. Construction began in 1920, although the work was not completed until 1953. The money, totaling $3 million, was raised solely by temple members as their gift to the peoples of the world.

The building has nine sides, each with an entrance door. Carved into the stone above the nine entrances, and above each of the nine alcoves, is a quote from Bah'u'llah, founder of the Baha'i faith. For the Baha'is the number nine, the largest single number, is a symbol of unity and oneness.

The simplicity of the Baha'i religion is reflected inside the temple. Rows of chairs fill the large auditorium, and only drapes hang from the walls—there are no altars, no pictures, no candles. From any seat one can view Lake Michigan, the gardens, or the quiet houses on Linden Avenue.

155 **Northwestern University Campus. 1851–.**
Sheridan Road between Clark and Lincoln streets, Evanston.

Founded in 1851, Northwestern University did not initially have a master plan for the design of its Evanston campus. Prairie School architect George Maher prepared such a plan in 1908, but the university never adopted its formal, axial pattern. Consequently, the buildings are rather randomly sited along the 4,000-foot stretch of lakeshore campus. The university's first building was constructed in 1855. Now demolished, it was a Greek revival structure of frame construction designed by John Mills Van Osdel, Chicago's first architect. The oldest campus building standing today is the 1869 University Hall, designed in a naive Gothic style. During the last three decades of the nineteenth century, a number of undistinguished, and largely unrelated, revival-style buildings were constructed. At the end of the first decade of this century, George Maher designed two campus buildings, in addition to his campus plan. Maher's Patten Gymnasium of 1909 (demolished 1940) was a powerful vaulted structure whose arched facade directly expressed the interior space. His Swift Hall, also of 1909, is in the best tradition of small Chicago school commercial structures.

One of the most prominent buildings on campus, by virtue of its location at the far side of a broad, open meadow, is the Deering Library of 1932. Designed by James Gamble Rogers, it is an example of the collegiate Gothic style popular for university campuses during the early twentieth century. Its superb siting was diminished in the early 1970s by the construction of Loebl, Schlossman, Bennett and Dart's Leverone Hall and School of Education, which interrupt the expanse of Deering Meadow and break the crescent configuration of the older buildings facing the meadow.

In 1961, the university decided to expand its campus to the east by building on landfill. Sixty-five additional acres were created between 1962 and 1964. In 1966, the Lindheimer Astronomical Observatory was built at the northeast corner of the landfill. Designed by Skidmore, Owings and Merrill, this almost sculptural composition consists of two domed observation towers clad in

sheet metal and joined by a bridge near the top. A trussed framework of steel tubing braces, supports, and unites the towers. The Core and Research Library of 1969 was also designed by Skidmore, Owings and Merrill. The three pavilions of reinforced concrete are connected at the base to each other and to the Deering Library. The configuration of the pavilions reflects the radial arrangement of the stacks and study carrels inside. The supporting concrete columns, projecting limestone panels, and narrow, vertical bands of windows create a vertical rhythm that animates the exterior. A performing arts center has also been built as part of this new campus.

156 Brown House. 1905.
2420 Harrison Street, Evanston.

Architect: Frank Lloyd Wright.

Throughout his life Frank Lloyd Wright was interested in the problem of low-cost housing for the middle-class family. He was never able to exercise his talent in this area to any great degree. Perhaps the nearest he came to solving the problem was in the Evanston model home built for Charles E. Brown in 1905.

This house is essentially the so-called four-square house that was developed from a design done for the *Ladies Home Journal* in 1901. Sometimes referred to as an economy Prairie house, this design and others like it were quite successful solutions to the small economical house problem. The Evanston model home was to serve as the first of a community of similar houses, but the project was never carried out.

157 Carter House. 1910. **NR**
1024 Judson Street, Evanston.

Architect: Walter Burley Griffin.

Walter Burley Griffin worked in the Oak Park studio of Frank Lloyd Wright for approximately five years. He established his own practice in 1907, after which he did a number of outstanding residences in Chicago and vicinity.

For several years Griffin's style was very similar to Wright's, but later his work showed more individuality. This house, which was built for Frederick B. Carter, Jr., in 1910, is reminiscent of Wright; but Griffin's signature is beginning to be seen in the heavier design elements and in the use of both brick and stucco, a combination Wright seldom employed. This house, like most of Griffin's designs, has the added advantage of a site completely landscaped by the architect. Griffin was an early advocate of professional landscape design, as well as an accomplished city planner.

158 Frank Lloyd Wright Home and Studio. NR
1889–95.

951 Chicago Avenue, Oak Park.

Architect: Frank Lloyd Wright.

Frank Lloyd Wright's house and studio, the construction of which began in 1889 (when Wright was only twenty-two) and continued for a period of more than six years, provide an interesting study in form and development. The house, facing Forest Avenue, was built first and is derivative of the Shingle style of the 1880s. Wright was still employed by Adler and Sullivan at the time and had not as yet developed his own style. It is interesting to note that Wright used several pieces of the ornamental castings from Adler and Sullivan's Auditorium Building, which was under construction at the same time, in the ceiling of his living room.

The studio, however, was built after Wright had established his own practice, and although it is connected to the house, it is a separate entity. The design anticipates Wright's work in the years after the turn of the century. The plan is a precursor of the open plans of the later years, and the use of materials reflects Wright's ideas at that time. The octagonal library was the last element added to the complex, which also includes a second-story, barrel-vaulted playroom added in 1893. Alterations to the house and studio were made over the years to accommodate several apartments. In 1974, the National Trust for Historic Preservation acquired the house and entered into an agreement with the Frank Lloyd Wright Home and Studio Foundation, whereby the foundation is responsible for the operation of the house and for restoring it to its appearance in 1909, the last year Wright lived there.

159 Unitarian Universalist Church and Parish House. (Unity Temple.) 1906. **NR**

Lake Street at Kenilworth Avenue, Oak Park.

Architect: Frank Lloyd Wright.

This monolithic concrete structure was Wright's solution to a problem presented by the low budget of the small Unitarian congregation of Oak Park, Illinois. Wright had used concrete previously in the E-Z Polish Factory in Chicago, and had suggested its use as early as 1894 when his first "Concrete Monolithic Bank" was designed.

Unity Temple is actually two spaces, Unity Church and a parish house, connected by a low link which serves as an entrance. Both main buildings are lighted by high wall windows or skylights featuring some of Wright's finest abstract glass designs. The auditorium is a cube with the pulpit set well into the space, giving a sense of closeness between the speaker and the parishioners.

The parish house is a small cube with wings extending from two sides to provide for classrooms and meeting spaces. In recent years the building has been refurbished and minor changes have been incorporated in the parish house; however, it is essentially unchanged from Wright's original design.

The ornamental concrete work of the exterior piers is repeated on each facade. This was accomplished in an economical and logical fashion through reuse of the carefully constructed wooden molds for each of six major walls. These molds were designed to coordinate the massive concrete ornament with the delicate glazing of the structure.

For this period of Wright's career, Unity Temple is a unique creation. No other building of similar character was completed until his California work twenty years later.

160 Mrs. Thomas H. Gale House. 1909. NR
6 Elizabeth Street, Oak Park.

Architect: Frank Lloyd Wright.

The house Frank Lloyd Wright designed for Mrs. Thomas H. Gale in 1909 remains as one of his most successful essays in small house design. The cantilevers, interlocking forms, and voids—each tied to the central fireplace core—all combine to demonstrate the ability of Wright to integrate simple shapes into a complex but superb whole. To some authorities it anticipates the spirit and character of the International style that was to develop in the next three decades.

This house can be favorably compared to any other of Wright's works, but it is most often considered as a companion to Fallingwater, built a quarter of a century later.

161 **Winslow House. 1893.** **NR**

515 Auvergne Place, River Forest.

Architect: Frank Lloyd Wright.

The William H. Winslow house was Frank Lloyd Wright's first independent commission. The house is highly reminiscent of the work of Louis Sullivan, particularly in the exterior, second-story frieze and in the fenestration. The planning is, for Wright, extremely formal and reflects a conservative attitude which the young architect had at this time.

This house has been well maintained and remains in excellent condition. The stable, or garage, to the rear of the house was built at the same time and is more of an anticipation of Wright's later style.

162 Drummond House. 1909. **NR**

559 Edgewood, River Forest.

Architect: William Drummond.

William Drummond, practicing both alone and with his partner, Louis Guenzel, was one of the most successful of the many persons trained by Frank Lloyd Wright in his Oak Park studio. In refining Wright's concept of the economical Prairie house in the design of his own house, he achieved an architectural gem.

The plan of the first floor is almost completely open with only the kitchen separated. The second floor is done in a conventional manner. Throughout, the house is furnished with pieces designed by Drummond, which contribute to the effect of livability.

163 Coonley House. 1908. **NR**

300 Scottswood, Riverside.

Architect: Frank Lloyd Wright.

The Avery Coonley house is in a class that includes only the very best of Frank Lloyd Wright's work—the Frederick C. Robie House and Unity Temple are perhaps the other prime examples in this category.

The Coonley House, in itself a large building, is but a part of an extensive complex which included a gardener's cottage, a garage building, formal gardens, a pool, a service court, and excellent landscaping throughout.

The house is designed with most of the principal rooms on a second level over a raised ground floor. The massing is extremely complex but forms a unified whole with nearly every portion liberally sprinkled with "Wrightian" ornament. The color scheme is dominated by earthen hues, but bits of brilliant red, green, and gold are used for emphasis throughout the house.

The grounds of the Coonley estate no longer exist in their original extent, having been largely disposed of for construction of new houses. Thus, the house now suffers from crowding by its neighbors.

Coonley House

164 **St. Procopius Abbey. 1970.**
5601 College Road, Lisle.

Architects: Loebl, Schlossman, Bennett and Dart.

Simplicity rather than austerity was the goal in the design of this Benedictine abbey. The late architect Edward Dart used broad, simple forms expressed in basic, natural materials such as wood and common brick. The dominant mass of the composition is the main church, which seats 800. Adjacent to it are a small chapel; dining, meeting, and recreation rooms; 100 sleeping rooms for the monks; guest rooms; and an infirmary, all arranged around a cloister garden. The abbey is handsomely sited on an 8-acre wooded hillside.

Bibliography

Andreas, A. T.
History of Chicago: From the Earliest Period to the Present Time. 3 vols. Chicago, 1884–86.

Useful for locations and dates of many buildings constructed before 1884; however, it rarely indicates architect.

Bach, Ira J.
Chicago on Foot. Revised 3d ed. Chicago: Rand McNally, 1977.

A series of walking tours of the city.

Blaser, Werner
Mies van der Rohe: The Art of Structure. New York: Frederick A. Praeger, 1965.

Brooks, H. Allen
The Prairie School: Frank Llyod Wright and His Midwest Contemporaries. Toronto: University of Toronto Press, 1973.

Chicago. Commission on Chicago Historical and Architectural Landmarks
Chicago Landmarks 1978. Chicago: City of Chicago, Commission on Chicago Historical Architectural Landmarks, 1978.

Documents the forty-one Chicago Landmarks that had been designed by the City Council of Chicago as of May 1978. The Commission also publishes informative, illustrated brochures on both designated and potential city landmarks.

Cohen, Stuart E.
Chicago Architects: Documenting the Exhibition of the Same Name Organized by Laurence Booth, Stuart E. Cohen, Stanley Tigerman, and Benjamin Weese. Chicago: Swallow Press, 1976.

Condit, Carl W.
Chicago, 1910–29: Building, Planning, and Urban Technology. Chicago: University of Chicago Press, 1973.

Condit, Carl W.
Chicago, 1930–70: Building, Planning, and Urban Technology. Chicago: University of Chicago Press, 1974.

Condit, Carl W.
The Chicago School of Architecture: A History of Commercial and Public Building in the Chicago Area, 1875–1925. Chicago: University of Chicago Press, 1964.

Drury, John
Old Chicago Houses. 1945. Reprint. Chicago: University of Chicago Press, 1975.

Each entry first appeared as part of a series in the *Chicago Daily News* during the 1930s. At that time few studies of old houses outside New England and the South had been done.

Eaton, Leonard K.
Two Chicago Architects and Their Clients: Frank Lloyd Wright and Howard Van Doren Shaw. Cambridge, Mass.: M.I.T. Press, 1969.

Giedion, Sigfried
Space, Time and Architecture: The Growth of a New Tradition. Cambridge, Mass.: Harvard University Press, 1954.

This modern classic, the scope of which extends far beyond architecture in Chicago, is included here because of the importance of its insight into nineteenth- and twentieth-century architecture and because of the excellent section on Chicago.

Grube, Oswald W.; Pran, Peter C.; and Schulze, Franz
100 Years of Architecture in Chicago: Continuity of Structure and Form. Chicago: J. Philip O'Hara, 1976.

Catalogue of an exhibition organized by Oswald Grube in 1973 for Die Neue Sammlung in Munich. Three years later, the exhibit was expanded and presented at the Museum of Contemporary Art in Chicago.

Hines, Thomas S.
Burnham of Chicago: Architect and Planner. New York: Oxford University Press, 1974.

Includes a list of buildings designed by Burnham.

Hoffman, Donald
The Architecture of John Wellborn Root. Baltimore: Johns Hopkins University Press, 1973.

Manson, Grant Carpenter
Frank Llyod Wright to 1910: The First Golden Age. New York: Van Nostrand Reinhold Company, 1958.

Mayer, Harold M., and Wade, Richard C.
Chicago: Growth of a Metropolis. Chicago: University of Chicago Press, 1969.

Moore, Charles H.
Daniel Burnham: Architect, Planner of Cities. 1921. Reprint (2 vols. in 1). New York: Da Capo Press, 1968.

Morrison, Hugh
Louis Sullivan, Prophet of Modern Architecture. 1935. Reprint. New York: Norton Library, 1962.

Randall, Frank A.
History of the Development of Building Construction in Chicago. Urbana: University of Illinois Press, 1949.

Probably the single most useful publication on building in an area slightly larger than the Loop. Despite an occasional error, the information on locations, dates, architects and engineers, costs, construction details, and references to illustrations is invaluable.

Randall, John D.
A Guide to Significant Chicago Architecture of 1872 to 1922. Glencoe, Ill.: Free Press, 1958.

Sullivan, Louis H.
The Autobiography of an Idea. New York: Press of the American Institute of Architects, 1924. Reprinted, New York: Dover Publications, 1956.

Written in the third person, this autobiography only goes up to 1893, the year of the World's Columbian Exposition.

Tallmadge, Thomas E.
Architecture in Old Chicago. 1941. Reprint. Chicago: University of Chicago Press, 1975.

Readable discourse on architecture, architects, and civic leaders.

Glossary

Caisson—An air chamber, resembling a well, driven down to firm foundation material and filled with concrete.

Cantilevered—Built with beams projected horizontally, supported by a downward force behind a fulcrum.

Capital—The element at the top of a column or of any other vertical support in a building.

Chamfered—With the edge where two surfaces meet in an exterior angle, reduced or rounded; beveled.

Chicago window—A window occupying the full width of the bay and divided into a large fixed sash flanked by a narrow movable sash at each side.

Colonnette—A small column, often used decoratively rather than functionally for support.

Corbel—A supporting form for a wall, consisting of layers or levels of masonry or wood, beyond the wall surface.

Corbel-tables—Successive corbels supporting a superstructure or upper moldings, beneath a spire or parapet, or below the eaves.

Cornice—The projecting member at the top of a wall; often a decorative development of the eaves of the roof.

Cupola—A terminal structure, rising above a main roof.

Dentils—A series of blocklike projections forming a molding, borrowed from the Greek Ionic style.

Facade—The face or front of a building.

Festoon—A decorative garland, sculptured in relief as a loop between two points.

Gable—The upper part of a terminal wall, under the ridge of a pitched roof.

Georgian—The architectural style developed during the reigns of Queen Anne and the four Georges, 1702–1830.

Gothic—The architecture of the thirteenth, fourteenth, and fifteenth centuries, characterized by the isolation of vertical thrusts of stone masonry, and the use of pointed arches, buttresses, and stone tracery.

Helical—In the form of a helix, a curve traced by a point moving in a circle as it simultaneously moves along a straight line.

Mannerist—Elaborate, highly stylized in the manner of the sixteenth- and seventeenth-century Italian painters.

Mansard—A roof having a shape in two planes, with the lower usually the steeper.

Masonry—Construction using plaster, concrete, and the application of stone, brick, tile, etc., with mortar.

Molding—Any interruption of the plane surface of a structure for the purpose of effecting a transition or for decorative effect.

Mullion—An upright division member between a series of windows or doors.

Nave—The main portion of a church or cathedral occupied by the worshipers, excluding the transepts.

Ornament—Detail applied to plain surfaces of a building, whether by sculpture, incising, painting, or any other method, for the purpose of embellishment.

Parapet—A low retaining wall at the edge of a roof, porch, or terrace.

Pier—Any upright structure used as a principal support by itself or as part of a wall.

Pilaster—An engaged pier of shallow depth.

Pile—A column driven into the ground as part of a foundation consisting of wood or concrete or concrete on top of wood.

Portico—An entrance porch.

Romanesque (or Norman)—Various styles of architecture, in vogue up to the twelfth century, and based on antique Roman forms.

Rosette—A circular floral motif, usually carved in stone.

Spandrel—The panel of wall between adjoining columns of a building and between the window sill above and the window head below it.

Spire—A tall tower roof, tapering up to a point.

String course—A continuous horizontal band, plain or molded, on an exterior wall.

Stucco—Plaster for exterior walls.

Terra-cotta—Cast and fired clay bricks, usually larger and more intricately modeled than bricks.

Transept—Either of the narrow side spaces, parallel to the nave and usually separated from it by columns, in a church of cruciform plan.

Truss—A combination of straight members arranged and connected so the stresses in the members, due to loads on the whole, are direct stresses; used for beam action over large spans.

Usonian—Term invented by Samuel Butler as an alternative to "American," in the sense of "pertaining to the United States," and applied by Frank Lloyd Wright to small, low-cost houses that he designed during the Depression.

Vaulted—Roofed by arched masonry, or having the appearance of a roof of arched masonry.

Window-hoods—A molding or decorative course immediately above a window which projects outward slightly from the main wall plane.

Credits

Bach, Ira J., 37, 63, 140
Cabanban, Orlando R., Cabanban Photo, 92
Chicago Aerial Survey, 198–99
Crane, Barbara, 9, 13–14, 18, 25, 26, 29, 31 (top), 43, 57, 67, 109, 110–15, 118, 123, 126, 156, 173, 177, 179–80, 191, 195, 197, 203–5
Goldberg, Bertrand, Associates, 149
Grubman, Steve, © Steve Grubman Photography, 165
Hale, Stephen, 117 (bottom), 143
Harr, Hedrich-Blessing, 151
Hedrich, Jim, Hedrich-Blessing, 101
Hedrich-Blessing, 74–75, 85, 87, 134, 162–63
Kalec, Don, 239
Lazan, Stanley M., 188
Loebl, Schlossman and Hackl, Inc., 247
Mallock, Roger, 193–94
Nelson, Harold A., 49, 155, 160, 174, 181, 207, 210, 213, 218, 227–29, 231, 233 (top), 234–35, 237, 240, 243–45
Nickel, Richard, 11, 27–28, 34–36, 38, 77, 117 (top), 172, 189, 192, 216
Norman, Phylane, 50, 53, 56, 73, 108, 132, 139, 219
Scott, L., 182–83
Siegel, Arthur, 19, 39, 116, 119, 159, 161, 178, 206, 211, 220–21
Sinkevitch, Alice A., 124
Stoller, Ezra, © ESTO, 89
Thall, Bob, 4, 6, 10, 17, 21, 31 (bottom), 33, 40–41, 44–46, 52, 55, 57–58, 60–62, 69, 81, 91, 95, 97, 99, 122, 129, 133, 135–36, 196, 214
Turner, Philip, ©, 7, 76, 79, 83, 93, 125, 145, 147–48, 166–67, 184, 208–9, 233 (bottom)
Weinstein, Michael Peter, 3, 23, 32, 65–66, 71, 82, 105, 107, 127, 130–31, 137, 141, 230, 242
Willett, Mike, 215
Wilson, Dan, 5, 15, 22, 47, 54, 70, 120–21, 138, 171, 175, 223

Index of Buildings

The date given in each entry is the date of completion.

Index of Architects

Commission on Chicago Historical and Architectural Landmarks